THE OWNERSHIP INCOME OF MANAGEMENT

National Bureau of Economic Research

FISCAL STUDIES

THE
OWNERSHIP INCOME
OF MANAGEMENT

WILBUR G. LEWELLEN

Purdue University

NATIONAL BUREAU OF ECONOMIC RESEARCH

NEW YORK 1971

Distributed by COLUMBIA UNIVERSITY PRESS

NEW YORK AND LONDON

Copyright © 1971 by National Bureau of Economic Research
All Rights Reserved

Library of Congress Card No. 71-11998
ISBN: 0-87014-222-4

Printed in the United States of America

Relation of the Directors to the Work and Publications of the National Bureau of Economic Research

1. The object of the National Bureau of Economic Research is to ascertain and to present to the public important economic facts and their interpretation in a scientific and impartial manner. The Board of Directors is charged with the responsibility of ensuring that the work of the National Bureau is carried on in strict conformity with this object.

2. The President of the National Bureau shall submit to the Board of Directors, or to its Executive Committee, for their formal adoption all specific proposals for research to be instituted.

3. No research report shall be published until the President shall have submitted to each member of the Board the manuscript proposed for publication, and such information as will, in his opinion and in the opinion of the author, serve to determine the suitability of the report for publication in accordance with the principles of the National Bureau. Each manscript shall contain a summary drawing attention to the nature and treatment of the problem studied, the character of the data and their utilization in the report, and the main conclusions reached.

4. For each manuscript so submitted, a special committee of the Board shall be appointed by majority agreement of the President and Vice Presidents (or by the Executive Committee in case of inability to decide on the part of the President and Vice Presidents), consisting of three directors selected as nearly as may be one from each general division of the Board. The names of the special manuscript committee shall be stated to each Director when the manuscript is submitted to him. It shall be the duty of each member of the special manuscript committee to read the manuscript. If each member of the manuscript committee signifies his approval within thirty days of the transmittal of the manuscript, the report may be published. If at the end of that period any member of the manuscript committee withholds his approval, the President shall then notify each member of the Board, requesting approval or disapproval of publication, and thirty days additional shall be granted for this purpose. The manuscript shall then not be published unless at least a majority of the entire Board who shall have voted on the proposal within the time fixed for the receipt of votes shall have approved.

5. No manuscript may be published, though approved by each member of the special manuscript committee, until forty-five days have elapsed from the transmittal of the report in manuscript form. The interval is allowed for the receipt of any memorandum of dissent or reservation, together with a brief statement of his reasons, that any member may wish to express; and such memorandum of dissent or reservation shall be published with the manuscript if he so desires. Publication does not, however, imply that each member of the Board has read the manuscript, or that either members of the Board in general or the special committee have passed on its validity in every detail.

6. Publications of the National Bureau issued for informational purposes concerning the work of the Bureau and its staff, or issued to inform the public of activities of Bureau staff, and volumes issued as a result of various conferences involving the National Bureau shall contain a specific disclaimer noting that such publication has not passed through the normal review procedures required in this resolution. The Executive Committee of the Board is charged with review of all such publications from time to time to ensure that they do not take on the character of formal research reports of the National Bureau, requiring formal Board approval.

7. Unless otherwise determined by the Board or exempted by the terms of paragraph 6, a copy of this resolution shall be printed in each National Bureau publication.

(Resolution adopted October 25, 1926, and revised February 6, 1933, February 24, 1941, and April 20, 1968)

CONTENTS

LIST OF TABLES

LIST OF CHARTS

ACKNOWLEDGMENTS

THE RESEARCH EFFORT described on the following pages has benefited greatly from the generous assistance of a number of individuals and organizations during the past several years. A particular debt is owed to Professor Daniel M. Holland of the Sloan School of Management at the Massachusetts Institute of Technology for his early and continuing help in formulating both objectives and strategy. The counsel of my colleagues at the Krannert Graduate School of Industrial Administration at Purdue University, Professors Robert W. Johnson and Blaine Huntsman, was invaluable throughout the investigation, as was the advice and encouragement of Professor John Lintner of the Harvard Graduate School of Business Administration. Conversations at various stages with V. Henry Rothschild II of New York City, Winthrop T. Lewis of the John Hancock Mutual Life Insurance Company in Boston, and Raymond J. Sullivan of the Public Reference Section of the Securities and Exchange Commission in Washington aided materially in refining the analysis and securing the necessary background information for its execution. Direct assistance with data collection and computer programming was provided by James Bauer of the Krannert School and Ira Miller of the Sloan School, both of whom performed in the capacity of research assistants at a level of competence substantially in excess of any reasonable expectation.

The staff of the National Bureau played a similarly vital role. Geoffrey Moore's initial support for the concept of the study was a pivotal factor, while the effective administration of the subsequent undertaking by Victor Fuchs smoothed the author's path considerably. Dr. Fuchs' suggestions ably complemented the incisive commentary of the Bureau's staff reading committee, comprised of William Landes, Richard Ruggles, and Neil Wallace, and the perceptive critique by Erwin D. Canham, George Cline Smith, and Robert J. Lampman of the Directors' reading committee. Additional contributions and suggestions were made by Eli Goldston and Emilio G. Collado. Special thanks is due also to Professor Robert Eisner of Northwestern University, whose very generous and very thorough review of the manuscript in its latter stages gave rise to a number of improvements in both style and content. Ruth Ridler's editorial expertise supplied the finishing touches.

The Bureau's financial resources were augmented with funds provided by the Purdue Research Foundation, the Krannert School, the Ford Foundation's Grant for Research in Business Finance to the Sloan School at M.I.T., and the Division of Research of the Harvard Business School. Dean John S. Day of Purdue, Dean William F. Pounds of M.I.T., and Dean Lawrence E. Fouraker of Harvard were especially generous in their support. The cooperation of the staff of Baker Library at Harvard also deserves prominent mention not only for permitting access to that institution's extensive collection of corporation records, but for making the actual process of data compilation as pleasant as any such task could be. The computations were performed at the computer centers of Purdue, M.I.T., and Harvard.

It must be emphasized, however, that the massive good fortune associated with being able to call upon the range of talents indicated does not necessarily imply a corresponding ability to translate that assistance into an effective end product. The analytical and expositional shortcomings which remain are unambiguously the responsibility of the author.

W. G. L.

1

INTRODUCTION

TRADITIONAL ECONOMIC ANALYSES of industrial behavior have as their foundation the proposition that the managers of an enterprise guide its activities in such a way as to maximize profits. The theory of the firm as developed in its conventional form depends heavily on the profit maximization presumption, and the alleged allocative efficiency of the private enterprise system is grounded on the market implications of that objective. If it should turn out, therefore, that profits are not pursued by firms very diligently in practice, the relevance of a substantial portion of our received economic and political doctrine would become suspect.

The possibility that in a complex and heavily industrialized society, certain other managerial goals may well take precedence has been raised in the literature with increasing frequency in recent years. This is especially true where the very large corporation is concerned. We are reminded at regular intervals, by both the popular and the scholarly press, that the era of the owner-executive has passed. The professional managers who nowadays run the several hundred major firms which set the pace in our contemporary economy are said to have become effectively insulated from the motivations provided by the monetary rewards—and stirrings of pride—characteristically attendant upon proprietorship. Instead, their circumstances are described in terms which suggest that such men might properly be viewed as the private sector's occupational counterparts of the apocryphal civil servant—secure employees of an immense organization who are apt to feel only an incidental identification with the interests and objectives of those whom the organization is, in principle, established to serve.

Whether one subscribes to this image or not, it is clear that the direct link between corporate performance and managerial rewards which was an essential feature of a simpler commercial environment consisting of a multitude of small entrepreneurs is no longer automatically present. We must, therefore, carefully consider the extent to which it is logical to count on the personal goals of management in publicly held enterprises being in harmony with the profit-maximizing desires of shareholders. If, indeed, no meaningful mechanism exists for eliciting such a congruence, neither the political nor the economic primacy of the free-market system can be proclaimed with the traditional vigor—and our economy's long-run productive performance may well fall short of the potential offered by an efficient allocation of resources.

The task of the analysis that follows is to appraise the possibility that an appropriate mechanism *is* present; to determine whether that mechanism seems sufficiently viable to encourage the sort of managerial behavior we desire; and to document the empirical dimensions of its impact. The question, in short, is whether the corporate environment, as presently constituted, contains an executive pay-off function that should lead to profit-maximizing managerial decisions, thereby validating the basic tenets of our normative economic models. The conclusion here will be that it does, and that the observably high degree of separation of ownership and management *roles* in the modern corporation has not been accompanied by a significant separation of their respective *self-interests*.

The Behavioral Possibilities

It is important to make explicit at the outset that only the economic incentives available to and experienced by contemporary professional managers will be considered in the subsequent discussion. No attempt will be made to investigate, or to assess, the multiple nonpecuniary channels through which individuals may seek job satisfaction. While organization theorists have correctly pointed out that such considerations may not only be influential in determining behavior but may, in fact, predominate in many instances, an adequate treatment of that possibility is beyond the competence of the present analysis. The entire concern here will be an attempt to uncover the nature, direction, and strength of the measurable *monetary* factors impinging upon the managers of the corporate enterprise. The conclusions drawn presuppose that additional personal income is, at least to some degree, relevant to and sought by business executives. Accordingly, the question is whether the source and form of that income should render an executive's attitudes toward his firm's market performance consistent with those of its shareholders. Since this contention is widely disputed, the issue involved appears of sufficient general concern to merit attention.[1] If, for example, it can be established that, in practice, professional managers maximize their own incomes when their firms have maximum profits, a powerful argument for anticipating the effective operation of the industrial system in this country will have been provided. The analysis of the nonpecuniary motivations of the same individuals can then proceed on substantially more solid ground and be framed with an appreciation of the strength of the underlying economic relationships which must be either supplemented or overcome. Indeed, unless and until we know more than we now do about those economic relationships, speculation as to *what else* executives might be influenced by in making their managerial decisions seems premature.

The Prevailing Economic View

Previous investigations of the character of executives' personal income links to their employer companies' success or failure [2] have arrived at conclusions which seem to fall consistently into two categories. On the one hand, the assertion is that those links are *too weak* to provide much impetus to efficient and diligent administration of the firm's affairs by its top management. The professional manager is depicted as being largely insulated from a meaningful regular job-performance

[1] Perhaps the most eloquent—and certainly the best-known—discussion of this broad area is contained in J. K. Galbraith, *The New Industrial State,* Boston, Houghton Mifflin, 1967.

[2] More precisely, it is *relative* success or failure which is at issue. Few sizeable corporations literally fail in the sense that they end up going out of business, but there are clearly a broad range of comparative profit results observable in the community each year.

review by shareholders and therefore able to protect his annual compensation from exposure to the sort of rigorous market test that the firm must confront externally. Among the studies which may be listed as adhering generally to this interpretation are the classic works of Berle and Means,[3] and of Gordon,[4] and the more recent analyses by Mason,[5] Williamson,[6] Larner,[7] and by Monsen, Chiu, and Cooley.[8] In particular, Berle and Means alerted us to the tendency for effective voting control of a large enterprise having a wide public stock distribution to pass into the hands of management—through mastery of the proxy voting mechanism. Larner confirmed their predictions and concluded that only about thirty of the two hundred largest nonfinancial corporations in the United States can still be classified as truly "owner-controlled." This being so, there might well be reason to wonder whether professional managers will be impelled to concentrate on traditional entrepreneurial profit objectives in formulating the operating policies for their firms.

The second—but complementary—view maintains that even insofar as a corporation's performance and its executives' incomes *are* linked, the extant relationship is perverse. Specifically, it is contended that interfirm differences in top executive remuneration are more closely associated with differences in total annual *sales* volumes than with differences in profit levels. As a consequence, professional managers are characterized as being interested primarily in pursuing additional sales—subject perhaps to some implicit requirement that the corresponding profit rates be "reasonable"—rather than as

[3] A. A. Berle and G. C. Means, *The Modern Corporation and Private Property,* New York, Macmillan, 1934.

[4] R. A. Gordon, "Ownership and Compensation as Incentives to Corporate Executives," *Quarterly Journal of Economics,* Vol. LIV, No. 2 (May 1940), pp. 455–473.

[5] E. S. Mason, "The Apologetics of Managerialism," *Journal of Business,* Vol. XXXI, No. 1 (January 1958), pp. 1–11.

[6] O. E. Williamson, *The Economics of Discretionary Behavior,* Englewood Cliffs, N.J., Prentice-Hall, 1964.

[7] R. J. Larner, "Ownership and Control in the 200 Largest Nonfinancial Corporations, 1929 and 1963," *American Economic Review,* Vol. LVI, No. 4 (September 1966), pp. 777–787.

[8] R. J. Monsen, J. S. Chiu, and D. E. Cooley, "The Effect of Separation of Ownership and Control on the Performance of the Large Firm," *Quarterly Journal of Economics,* Vol. LXXXII, No. 3 (August 1968), pp. 435–457.

attempting to increase profits per se. By adopting this strategy, they are presumably following a course which will most effectively augment their own incomes. The rationale for such a position has been developed by Baumol,[9] Marris,[10] and Williamson,[11] and a certain amount of allegedly corroborative evidence has been offered by Roberts,[12] and by McGuire, Chiu, and Elbing.[13] Not surprisingly, their analyses suggest that the pattern of industrial behavior and the nature of the process of resource allocation in the community will differ in several important respects from the classical result if higher sales, instead of higher profits, are the main economic concern of corporate management.[14]

Rebuttal

The intention in these pages is not to deny the facts of ownership-management separation and the emergence of professional administrators, nor to dispute the ability of executives to exercise practical voting control of their firms through proxy solicitations. Rather, the

[9] W. J. Baumol: "On the Theory of Oligopoly," *Economica*, Vol. XXV, No. 99 (August 1958), pp. 187–198; "On the Theory of Expansion of the Firm," *American Economic Review*, Vol. LII, No. 5 (December 1962), pp. 1078–1087; *Business Behavior, Value, and Growth*, New York, Macmillan, 1967.

[10] R. Marris, *The Economic Theory of Managerial Capitalism*, New York, Free Press, 1964.

[11] J. Williamson, "Growth, Sales, and Profit Maximization," *Economica*, Vol. XXXIII, No. 129 (February 1966), pp. 1–16.

[12] D. R. Roberts, *Executive Compensation*, New York, Free Press, 1959.

[13] J. W. McGuire, J. S. Chiu, and A. O. Elbing, "Executive Incomes, Sales, and Profits," *American Economic Review*, Vol. LII, No. 4 (September 1962), pp. 753–761.

[14] Given the likelihood that nonpecuniary job goals are also relevant to executives, it should of course be stressed that "sales maximization" is not necessarily quite an appropriate description of the hypothesis advanced by the writers cited. Thus, management may well be thought of as seeking increased sales in preference to all other measurable indices of company performance— but may not address even that result with full vigor if it interferes substantially with the realization of various subjective job satisfactions. The same comment applies to the use herein of the term "profit maximization." The latter should be interpreted simply as denoting the *primacy* of profits among the operating economic goals of management, if not literally the squeezing out of the last possible profit dollar regardless of the noneconomic personal sacrifices perceived by executives.

objective will be to present some new empirical evidence about the economic circumstances of senior corporate officials which argues strongly that the phenomena indicated have not been sufficient to create a real difference between the pecuniary interests of management and stockholders. The claim will be that the relevant executive pay-off functions still have the right form to encourage profit-seeking behavior as the dominant pattern, despite the pervasive separation of ownership and control. Put differently, to the degree that increments to their personal income are of interest to professional managers, higher corporate profits can be shown to produce those increments more directly and more consistently than any other vehicle under executive jurisdiction.

The basis for these assertions is found in two key features of the contemporary corporate executive's relationship to his company which have, to date, been given insufficient attention in the literature. First, his compensation for services rendered does not consist merely of those stable direct annual cash payments called salary and bonus, which are invariably used as measures of his earnings. In fact, the senior executive compensation package turns out to have been weighted quite heavily in recent years toward what may be classed as contingent "ownership" items of one kind or another—arrangements which utilize shares of the employer corporation's common stock as the compensation medium, and whose ultimate value necessarily depends on the securities market's response to the firm's achievements. Second, while it is true that nowadays there are very few large, publicly held companies in which the top management group holds a majority or even a substantial minority of the outstanding stock, it is nonetheless also true that the stockholdings which executives *do* have are sufficiently large that the economic impact of those holdings is highly important in the context of executives' *personal* wealth positions. Thus, we shall see that the income which the typical upper-level professional manager enjoys each year from the combination of such items of remuneration as stock bonuses, stock options, and profit-sharing plans, plus the dividends and capital gains occasioned by his holdings of his company's shares, bulks large in comparison with—indeed, dominates—receipts from salaries, cash bonuses, pension promises, and other traditional "fixed-dollar" rewards. Consequently, we find that the ownership-management earnings link is not so tenuous after all. The possibility—or, more precisely, the likelihood—of a continuing close identification by executives with the profit objectives of shareholders thereupon seems more plausible than the conventional view suggests.

Profits and Stock Prices

Before proceeding, however, one important—if not very original—point should be emphasized. Implicit in the following discussion is the proposition that, as managerial goals, "profit maximization" and "share price maximization" for a firm are equivalent concepts. When properly defined, the latter is simply a more rigorous and more comprehensive restatement of the former in situations where it is necessary to deal not only with the anticipated *size* of the elements in a stream of corporate earnings, but with their *futurity* and *uncertainty* as well. In the last decade or so, the theoretical literature concerned with corporate investment and financing decisions has, of course, established this principle as the core of the normative decision-making framework.[15] Hence, in addressing the relevant issues, the position throughout will be that shareholders and management can be considered to share a common economic goal whenever management's personal income depends significantly on either the firm's profits or the market-price behavior of its common stock.

[15] See, for example: F. and V. Lutz, *The Theory of Investment of the Firm*, Princeton, Princeton University Press, 1951; D. Durand, "Costs of Debt and Equity Funds for Business: Trends and Problems of Measurement," *Conference on Research in Business Finance*, New York, National Bureau of Economic Research, 1952, pp. 215–247; F. Modigliani and M. H. Miller, "The Cost of Capital, Corporation Finance, and the Theory of Investment," *American Economic Review*, Vol. XLVIII, No. 3 (June 1958), pp. 261–297; M. J. Gordon, *The Investment, Financing, and Valuation of the Corporation*, Homewood, Illinois, Richard D. Irwin, 1962; J. Lintner, "Optimal Dividends and Corporate Growth Under Uncertainty," *Quarterly Journal of Economics*, Vol. LXXVIII, No. 1 (February 1964), pp. 49–95; J. Lintner, "The Valuation of Risk Assets and the Selection of Risky Investments in Stock Portfolios and Capital Budgets," *Review of Economics and Statistics*, Vol. XLVII, No. 1 (February 1965), pp. 13–37.

Background of the Study

The origins of the present investigation lie in a recently published empirical study of executive compensation policies in large, publicly held corporations, conducted by the author, also for the National Bureau of Economic Research.[16] In that undertaking, a record was constructed of the value to a representative group of senior executives of all the major items in their compensation packages: pension benefits, stock options, stock bonuses, stock purchase plans, deferred-pay arrangements, and profit-sharing plans, as well as salaries and cash bonuses. The resultant figures were cast in the form of an annual measure of total after-tax remuneration for each executive in question for each relevant year of his employment experience. The output, therefore, provides both a comprehensive historical index of aggregate managerial reward and a profile of its constituents.[17] Those analytical techniques and computational procedures developed that bear on the current effort will be summarized below, but the reader is, of course, referred to the original volume for a full description.

The data for the investigation were obtained from the proxy statements which corporations must submit in connection with their annual shareholders' meetings. The Securities and Exchange Commission requires that the main features of the compensation arrangements enjoyed by the senior officials of a firm be reported.[18] In addition, holdings of the corporation's securities by individuals serving on its board of directors must be listed. Since, in practice, most top-level administrators are also members of the board, it became evident while gathering the data for the compensation study that sizeable ownership positions in their firms were not unusual among executives. In fact, the stock holdings observed, while invariably far from denoting significant voting interests, were sufficiently large in many instances

---

[16] W. G. Lewellen, *Executive Compensation in Large Industrial Corporations,* New York, National Bureau of Economic Research, 1968.

[17] See also: Leonard R. Burgess, *Top Executive Pay Package,* New York, Free Press, 1963.

[18] Specifically, the requirement now is that information be presented for the three highest-paid officers and for any director who earns more than $30,000 a year.

to suggest that the annual income accruing therefrom in the form of dividends and capital gains might be as, or more, important to the men involved as their reported remuneration as employees. This impression reinforced the finding in the compensation analysis that ownership-related instruments of remuneration have themselves come to comprise a significant percentage of total managerial pay. The possibility, then, that there existed a much stronger, more direct, and more rational ownership-management income link than was generally recognized prompted the current study.

Focus

When combined with the indicated data on compensation, and with information on corporations' stock prices and per-share dividend payments over time, the proxy statement reports of stockholdings permit a detailed reconstruction of top management's historical ownership experience in several dimensions. In terms of our interest here, the market value of the designated holdings and, as suggested, a comparison between the periodic dividends received and capital gains enjoyed by executives on the one hand, and their employee compensation on the other, seem the most pertinent aspects of that experience. The investigation will, therefore, concentrate on exploring these elements of the record.

The roster of firms whose executives' circumstances are examined consists of three different and distinct groups: fifty very large manufacturing corporations, fifteen companies engaged in retail trade, and fifteen small manufacturers. The large manufacturers comprise the sample which was analyzed in the original compensation study. They were drawn from the top of *Fortune* magazine's tabulation of the five hundred largest United States industrials for the year 1963.[19] Some fifteen industry categories appear on the list, and the firms involved averaged $1.9 billion in sales, $1.6 billion in assets, and $130 million in after-tax profits during 1963. Taken together, they accounted for roughly one-fourth of the total sales of the entire manu-

[19] *Fortune,* Vol. 70, No. 1 (July 1964), pp. 179–198.

facturing sector. As such, their executives' experience may legitimately be considered representative of the situation in the large, publicly held enterprise in this country.

The retail trade and small manufacturing samples are completely new, and are offered here as a counterpoint to the findings for the large manufacturers. The former grouping includes what are, for all practical purposes, the fifteen largest retailers in the country and encompasses virtually every nationwide chain of stores currently operating. The small manufacturing sample was compiled from the companies ranked 350th and below on *Fortune's* list. On average, they had $118 million of sales, $85 million of assets, and $5 million of after-tax profits in 1963. These figures suggest that, while some fairly decent-sized corporations are in fact counted within the group, they are clearly cut from a different cloth and function at a much smaller scale of operations than the corresponding large manufacturers. Useful comparisons among the findings for the three samples should, therefore, be possible.

The investigation will cover the period 1940 to 1963 in all three instances, this being the interval for which the underlying large manufacturing compensation data were generated. Nineteen-forty should constitute a sensible starting point in any case, since that year just precedes the current era of high progressive marginal personal tax rates and thus allows the historical record to reflect the important environmental changes which have occurred. Approximately 950 different individual executives and some 8700 man-years of earnings and ownership evidence are included in the computations.

Organization

In Chapter 2, the basis of selection—as well as the particular characteristics—of the three samples will be discussed, and the procedures employed in their analysis described. Chapter 3 presents the relevant data on executive compensation for all three groups, while Chapters 4 through 6 offer accounts of top management's ownership experience for each sample in turn. Chapter 7 summarizes the findings and outlines the conclusions which those results suggest.

The Findings

Among the major elements in the historical record which emerges are the following:

1. In recent years, the senior executives of the country's largest industrial corporations have owned an average of between $1 million and $2 million worth of their respective companies' common stock *per capita*.
2. In terms of market values, these figures represent a threefold to fourfold increase in ownership since the early 1940's.
3. The annual dividends and capital gains occasioned by the holdings are well in excess of the amounts the same individuals receive in the form of compensation as employees of the firms in question.
4. When those dividends and gains are added to the stock-related compensation of executives, the resulting totals run anywhere from three to five times the value of the corresponding fixed-dollar rewards from salary, cash bonuses, pensions, and similar items.
5. This degree of ownership involvement actually surpasses that observable among the executives of smaller firms, despite the prevailing view that large companies are the ones wherein the problem of the separation of management and ownership is most severe.
6. The annual income enjoyed by the senior officers of small industrial enterprises and of retailing organizations is, on the other hand, also highly dependent on the dividends and stock price performance of the various employer corporations. As such, it offers compelling evidence of a broad-based link in the economy between managerial wealth and shareholder returns.

The particulars of these findings are spelled out in subsequent chapters, and their relationship to the matter of likely executive decision rules is considered. It should be emphasized again, however, that only measurable economic phenomena are at issue. While it may be reasonable in places to draw some inferences about possible managerial responses to the evidence uncovered, it will in no sense be legitimate to contend that a solid behavioral model has been provided. The more modest hope is that the data presented will enhance our understanding of the relevant environment, and will offer some improved documentation of the income consequences and opportunities confronting the professional manager.

2

THE METHODOLOGY
AND THE DATA

THE MOST APPROPRIATE FRAME of reference for an analysis of the ownership-related income of senior corporate executives is a comparison with the remuneration they receive in their capacity as employees. Accordingly, a brief summary of the procedures utilized in arriving at the findings of the initial compensation study seems in order. It will also serve as an introduction to the methodology of the current investigation, since the same procedures have been extended to the two additional samples examined here. The techniques adopted in generating measures of annual ownership income, and in relating the various earnings flows to each other, will be seen to follow directly from the original analytical framework.

The Compensation Figures

As indicated earlier, the motive for undertaking the compensation study was to improve upon the prevailing empirical treatment of executive pay, which implicitly assumed that salary and bonus payments alone provided an adequate index of remuneration for purposes of drawing conclusions about inter-company or inter-industry patterns of reward. The rapid growth in popularity of several key forms of deferred and contingent compensation during the years immediately following World War II suggested, however, that a more comprehensive approach might well be required if developments in corporate policy were to be appraised properly. With that in mind, the objective established was to develop and apply a set of techniques which would permit measurement of the remuneration furnished by *all* the major items in the managerial pay package. The intention was that this be accomplished in a manner that would not only allow the resulting values to be compared meaningfully but would produce a workable figure for total annual compensation.

The magnitude of the income accruing to an individual in a given year from his salary and bonus earnings was easily determined, simply by subtracting from the observed pre-tax amounts the relevant statutory personal income tax liability for the year. The latter must reflect the deductions and exemptions from taxable income which the man is likely to claim, but estimates of those quantities, by income bracket, were obtainable from IRS *Statistics of Income* tabulations.

A more imaginative approach was necessary in connection with rewards which had more complex timing, taxation, and contingency features. For each such "noncurrent" instrument, the valuation framework consisted of specifying what was denoted its "current income equivalent." This concept was defined to be the amount of additional current income—additional salary and bonus, if you will—which would be as valuable, after taxes, to the executive in question as the particular arrangement being considered. In effect, the hypothesis was that the most useful way to go about measuring on a common scale the compensation provided by the disparate supplements to direct cash payments to executives was to calculate the size of the cash increments which, if *substituted* for those supplements, would leave the men involved equally well off. "Equally well off" was, of course, perceived in after-tax terms.

As an illustration, in the case of a pension plan the question was asked: How much of an increase in annual after-tax salary would the prospective pension recipient require in order to be able to purchase therewith an individual retirement annuity from an insurance company which would be similar in form and equal in value to the benefits promised him under his corporation's retirement plan? The indicated annual premium payments to the insurer were taken to be the "after-tax current income equivalent" of the man's pension expectations. They measure very precisely the amount of additional immediate cash income he would need in order to meet the purchase price of an alternative market instrument guaranteeing him the same level of economic security in retirement that his pension was designed to provide. By extension, the increase in his annual *pre-tax* salary which would have produced the required after-tax increments was interpreted as the pension's "before-tax current income equivalent."

While pension promises were especially easy to handle in such a framework due to the existence of a close market substitute readily available to an individual executive, other supplementary compensation arrangements were amenable to valuation by essentially the same approach. The current income equivalent of a post-retirement deferred pay contract, for example, was defined as that stream of annual payments which, if begun in the year the contract was entered into and continued up to retirement age, would have an after-tax present value matching that of the prospective deferred payments themselves. The equivalent of a stock option was specified to be a series of cash increments spread over the formal term of the option and having a value equal to the difference—net of capital gains taxes—between the option price of the shares involved and their market price on the date the option was exercised by its recipient. Similar procedures were employed in valuing the other components of the pay package. The result is a set of indices of remuneration which permit convenient and accurate statements about the absolute magnitude and relative importance of a group of originally quite different rewards.

The details of those procedures are sufficiently extensive that the interested reader is referred to the original treatise for their complete description.[1] An illustration of the kind of profile of the managerial pay package which emerges from their application to a typical individual's experience will be provided below. For present purposes, however, it should be enough to stress that in designing the relevant valuation techniques, the following principles were adhered to throughout: (1) "Equivalence" between a series of hypothetical increments to current income on the one hand, and the benefits anticipated from a given deferred or contingent compensation arrangement on the other, was always defined in terms of the after-tax present values of the two streams of payments. (2) The current income equivalent amounts were established according to that approach by

---

[1] Lewellen, *op. cit.,* see especially Chapters 2 through 6.

Nevertheless, to avoid being too cavalier, in the case of these percentages and each of the other parameters indicated, a thorough sensitivity analysis was performed to test the likelihood that the compensation figures generated might depend significantly on the particular parametric values incorporated in the computations. The clear conclusion was that any meaningful set of substitute choices—e.g., doubling the two discount rates to 5 and 10 per cent per annum after taxes— would have had little impact on either the historical trends or cross-sectional patterns which emerged. The saving feature of the situation turned out to be the fact that most assumptions influenced *both* sides of the many compensation-benefits vs. current-income-equivalent equations to just about the same extent, thus creating offsetting effects on the earnings measures produced.[7]

Coverage

Given the framework described, the only noteworthy items of remuneration that had to be excluded from the empirical analysis for lack of sufficient information were life and medical insurance programs and executive expense accounts. Corporate proxy statements do not list the benefit structures or receipts enjoyed by individual officers under either category of reward. Fortunately, for executives at the level we will be concerned with here, such devices should not bulk large in the compensation totals nor should their absence compromise the usefulness of the findings.[8] With these minor exceptions, it was

[7] For example, if a 5 per cent discount rate were used in calculating the present value of an executive's pension expectations instead of a 2½ per cent figure, the same 5 per cent rate should be adopted in finding the individual retirement annuity whose purchase would provide a matching present value. Since it necessarily is the comparison *between* the resulting present value figures rather than their respective absolute magnitudes which establishes "equivalence" in this manner, a fairly wide range of discount rates will, if applied simultaneously to both sides, yield roughly the same answers. See Lewellen, *op. cit.,* Chapter 12, for the details.

[8] Support for this contention in connection with expense accounts can be found in C. A. Hall, Jr., *Effects of Taxation on Executive Compensation and Retirement Plans,* Cambridge, Massachusetts, Riverside Press, 1951, where he states on p. 14 that: "According to executives interviewed, company-paid-for expenses of the type which really reduce executives' buying costs and repre-

possible for the large manufacturing companies—and *is* possible for the retailing and small manufacturing firms—to develop a good chronological record of the size and composition of the senior corporate executive pay package dating back to the year 1940. Since the SEC and its proxy statement reporting requirements are both relatively recent phenomena, consistently reliable and comprehensive information for earlier periods is simply not available.

Application

A concrete illustration of the kind of output which is generated when the computational procedures outlined are applied to a particular executive's employment circumstances is provided in Appendix A. As can be seen from that illustration, the analytical framework adopted requires a very "personalized" approach to valuation. In order to appraise an executive's rewards, his age and marital status must be known, and data on his compensation must be processed, from the moment he first becomes eligible for benefits under any of his firm's important deferred or contingent pay plans. It is these requirements which dictate that only the rewards of those men whose earnings histories are reported on in corporate proxy statements can be analyzed; such documents are the sole public repositories of information on the pay of particular individuals. This explains why the concern here will be exclusively with the topmost segment of the managerial hierarchy.

Stock Ownership Data

Those same executives' stockholdings in their own companies comprise the other—and at the moment, more important—portion of the story. As was indicated above, the possibility that the income consequences of senior corporate officers' equity investments in their employer firms might be quite substantial was raised by a casual inspection of stock ownership positions while the initial data on com-

sent extra income are of negligible importance in large companies." Admittedly, the age of this finding may by now cast some doubt on its credibility, but no more recent evidence seems to be available.

pensation were being collected. Upon completion of that effort, a more careful appraisal of the dimensions and implications of the owner- ship phenomenon—as well as an extension of the entire analysis to a broader range of enterprises—seemed a logical next step.

The approach was simply to go through the appropriate proxy statements and record, for each man whose circumstances were of interest, the number of shares of his company's common stock that he owned at the beginning of every year for which compensation data had been compiled.[9] The published figures pertain to those securities which are either directly or beneficially owned by the executive and his immediate family. An example of beneficial ownership, as inter- preted by the SEC, would be a situation in which shares are tempo- rarily held in trust for the man in question under an arrangement calling for his receipt of the annual dividends thereon and for the subsequent distribution of the shares to him upon, say, the demise of a relative. Alternatively, the securities might be nominally owned by a private holding company, which in turn would be controlled by the man and his family. In either case, the pecuniary rewards and contingencies of a direct ownership position are effectively transmitted to the individual executive, and the shares at issue properly considered a part of his total portfolio. However, the vast majority of stock- holdings observed empirically were owned outright by the men in the sample.

On the other side of the coin, the "immediate family" definition noted encompasses only the executive, his wife, and their unmarried children. The likelihood, therefore, is that the resulting data somewhat understate the true intensity of management's ownership involvement. Securities held by married children and by other fairly close family members are excluded—and these could, of course, be sizeable on occasion. The omissions are worth pointing out. They imply that a more comprehensive set of figures, were it available, would necessarily identify additional holdings whose influence would reinforce many of the conclusions offered here.

[9] Employer-company preferred stock and/or bond holdings by executives were not included in the investigation, both because they were of negligible size in the aggregate, and because, in principle, it is the identification of executives with *common stockholder* interests which is at issue here.

Since most senior corporate executives are also members of their respective firms' boards of directors, the proxy statement information on directors' stock ownership makes it possible to obtain data for all but a very few men whose compensation places them among their companies' top employees. In situations where the proxy statement listings are inadequate, a secondary source of information is the monthly SEC publication *Official Summary of Security Transactions and Holdings*.[10] This document contains a record of the securities owned—again, either directly or beneficially—by corporate officers and directors who buy or sell any of their firms' common or preferred shares within a given thirty-day period. While the data frequently lag behind the actual transactions by several months, for purposes of an historical analysis an executive can often be located among those tabulations for the years during which he was an officer but not yet a director.[11] In all, reliable annual stock ownership figures could be compiled for fully 552 of the 558 men who comprised the original large-manufacturing compensation sample, and for every one of the nearly 400 additional highly paid executives in the small-manufacturing and retail trade samples. The characteristics of each of these three groups will be discussed below.

Computational Framework

When the resulting stockholding data are supplemented by records of past share prices and corporate dividend declarations, a variety of elements of senior management's secular ownership experience may be examined. By the nature of our objectives, the market value of the indicated holdings at particular points in time, the capital gains and losses to which the individuals involved were subjected, and the cash dividends they received would appear to be the most significant components of that experience.

Since corporations report the relevant stock ownership positions every year, it is both a logical undertaking and an easy task to con-

---

[10] U.S. Securities and Exchange Commission, Washington, D.C., Government Printing Office.

[11] The same tabulations also assisted in identifying the dates of stock option exercises by executives as part of the compensation investigation.

struct an annual record of the market value of top executives' equity investments in their own firms. The first of the year seems a convenient valuation date, and the figures generated in subsequent chapters therefore are produced by multiplying the number of shares of his company's common stock owned by the executive as of January 1 of each year by the corresponding January 1 market price per share.[12] Because certain firms list directors' stockholdings for other dates, the *Official Summary of Transactions* bulletin cited above was used, where necessary, to retrace the relevant data to the start of the year.

The annual capital gains and losses associated with the observed holdings can, of course, take two forms: realized gains and so-called "paper" gains. The combined consequences of both should, in the view here, be recognized as important to a determination of the total effective ownership income of top executives—since quite clearly both can contribute to substantial changes in an individual's personal net worth. This contention is reinforced by the opportunity which is always available for investors to realize indirectly whatever paper gains they may enjoy by pledging the securities whose value has appreciated as collateral for personal loans. Accordingly, an executive's aggregate capital gain or loss as recorded for a particular year is computed by adding to his realized profits or losses from sales of his corporation's common stock during that year the increase or decrease in the market value from January 1 to December 31 of any shares he held *throughout* the year.

In order to properly implement this accrual approach to valuation and measurement, it was necessary in each instance to define the appropriate annual magnitudes in such a way as to avoid double-counting. This was accomplished by treating as the relevant *realized* gain for the year in question only the difference between the selling price of the shares disposed of and their immediately preceding January 1 market price. Thus, a significant fraction of many of the realized gains experienced by the men in the sample end up being parceled out

---

[12] Actually, due to the New Year holiday, December 31 closing prices were employed instead. The data were collected from back issues of the *Wall Street Journal* and the *Commercial and Financial Chronicle*.

here as accrued gains attributable to prior periods. By the same token, the paper gain tabulated for stock which is observed to be acquired after the beginning of a given year but held at least until the start of the following year is set equal to the difference between the purchase price of the shares and their market price on the succeeding December 31. These procedures provide both a consistent and comprehensive annual record of the capital appreciation patterns at issue.[13]

As a means of keeping the data collection and programming effort required within manageable bounds, however, an approximation to these procedures was decided upon in the execution of the analysis, especially where share prices were concerned. To avoid having to take into account individually all of the various stock transactions engaged in by the some 950 men in the three samples over the quarter-century period studied, the assumption was made instead that all purchases and sales took place at a price *midway* between the opening and closing prices of the year in which the transaction occurred.

For example, if an executive were found to own five-thousand shares of his firm's stock on January 1, 1960, their market value then being $20 per share, and six-thousand shares on December 31 at a price of $30 each, he was assumed to have acquired the observed difference of one-thousand shares at a cost of $25 per share during the year. His total capital gain was therefore defined to be $55,000—the imputed result of a $10 per share increment on five-thousand shares, plus a $5 gain on one-thousand shares. Without this simplification, the data needs for the study would have quickly gotten out of hand because of the sheer number of man-years of experience involved, despite the fact that the great majority of senior executives really undertake very little short-term trading in their employer com-

---

[13] To illustrate: Consider the case of an executive who purchases 1000 shares of his company's common stock during 1960 and resells them in 1962. Let us assume that the purchase price was $50 per share; the December 31, 1960, price $60 per share; the December 31, 1961, price $70; and the eventual selling price $80. Pursuant to the computational framework adopted here, the over-all realized profit of $30,000 before taxes would be divided up as an accrued capital gain of $10,000 for the year 1960, an accrued gain of $10,000 for 1961, and a realized gain of $10,000 for 1962. The corresponding measurements for any shares both bought and sold *within* a single year, of course, are clear-cut.

panies' shares.[14] There is no reason to suspect that, in the aggregate, any bias is thereby introduced into the findings or that any important information is lost.[15] The necessary share price adjustments for stock splits and stock dividends are, of course, built into the computations.

Executives' cash dividend receipts are estimated in a similar manner. If a man's stockholdings are seen to change during a particular year, the convention is that he received just half the total reported cash dividend payments by the firm for that year on the *incremental* shares. In the example cited above, then, if the corporation's 1960 dividend rate had been $1 per share, the executive described would have been credited with a total pre-tax dividend income of $5500, this consisting of $1 each on five-thousand shares added to 50 cents per share on one-thousand shares. In cases where stock dividends are declared, a complementary approximation is employed. The assumption is that the additional shares are distributed to the man halfway through the relevant year, causing his cash dividend receipts to be higher to that extent over the second six months. By this procedure, a 4 per cent stock dividend is translated into aggregate cash dividend flows amounting to 102 per cent of the reported per-share figure for the year.

Compensation and Ownership Income

It should be stressed that in all the foregoing calculations, a careful separation is maintained between the *compensation* which is generated in particular periods for the executive by such arrangements as stock bonuses and stock options on the one hand, and the man's subsequent *investment* income from his continued ownership of the shares thus acquired on the other. Once those shares are formally conveyed to him by his firm under a stock bonus plan, for instance, the compensa-

---

[14] For documentation, see below, pp. 107–108.

[15] Thus, it would seem that possible errors in the attendant stock price estimates are as apt to be on the high as the low side of the true values in any given situation. They may, in consequence, be expected to balance out for the sample as a whole. Indirect support for this contention can be found in C. E. Edwards and J. G. Hilton, "A Note on the High-Low Price Average as an Estimator of Annual Average Stock Prices," *Journal of Finance,* Vol. XXI, No. 1 (March 1966), pp. 112–115.

tion aspect of the interchange is regarded here as finished. Similarly, the option agreement—and the process of measuring the magnitude of the attendant remuneration—is treated as being terminated on the date the option recipient exercises his right to purchase the specified securities. The difference between the market price of the securities at that point and the stated option price the man pays definitively establishes his reward.[16] Any dividend earnings or capital gains experienced thereafter from any of these holdings clearly occur as a result of the executive's decision to retain the securities in his portfolio and to pursue the associated investment in his company. Because those flows are not logically a part of the compensation transaction, they are grouped here with the ownership income attributable to other stockholdings. This distinction is worth bearing in mind in interpreting the subsequent findings.

Tax Liabilities

On the presumption that the capital gains realized by senior corporate executives from trading in their own firms' common shares are predominantly long-term in nature,[17] a reasonable first approximation of the applicable tax liabilities thereon would be a flat 25 per cent. In almost every case, such men have incomes large enough to lead them, when the issue arises, to choose this "alternative" tax computation in preference to including half their capital gains with inflows taxable at regular statutory rates.[18] In the present context, however, it is necessary to specify the implicit tax liabilities on *accrued* as well as on actually realized gains if the hoped-for annual record of executives' ownership income is to be made meaningful in after-tax terms for purposes of a comparison with compensation. Because the payment of such taxes is, of course, deferred to the date the securities in

[16] The mechanics of translating that figure into a "current income equivalent" for the option are described in Lewellen, *op. cit.,* Chapter 4.

[17] Again, see pp. 107–108 below.

[18] For example, during the period 1954 to 1963 which comprised the last ten years of the empirical analysis, 25 per cent was the pertinent capital gains tax rate for any individual whose taxable income exceeded $32,000. Very few executives in the sample fell below that level.

question are sold rather than being levied on the accrual basis used here to measure many of the pre-tax gains which are of interest, some adjustment for the consequences of deferral is required. In addition, there is always the possibility that a portion of the relevant gains will turn out to be so long-term as to escape income taxation entirely— i.e., the securities may be retained in the executive's portfolio until he dies, in which circumstance no capital gains tax on the accrued profits would be paid.

For these reasons, 15 per cent was adopted as an estimate of the "true" over-all effective rate and was applied uniformly in the calculations to both realized and accrued annual before-tax capital gains. The choice was arbitrary, and was designed merely to remove in a convenient manner at least some part of what would otherwise obviously have been a persistent bias toward attributing too high a tax liability to the observed gains had the nominal 25 per cent figure been used. The reader is asked to interpret the choice in that spirit.[19] As it happens, just about *any* figure between zero and 25 per cent could be employed as far as the conclusions reached in the following chapters are concerned, since the important comparisons, as we shall see, are quite insensitive to the particular tax rate chosen in the

[19] As a rough guide, the feeling was that 15 per cent would be a reasonable approximation of the resulting average tax rate if one-fifth of the executives in the sample passed on their stockholdings in their estates—thereby reducing the average rate from 25 to 20 per cent—and, further, if in the face of an after-tax annual discount rate of 5 per cent, the mean length of time for the remaining individuals between the accrual and the realization of their capital gains were five years. Hence, the discount factor $1/(1.05)^5$ will diminish the effective present value of a tax liability on a gain accrued currently by about one-fourth, and lower an implied 20 per cent tax rate to 15 per cent. While basing the decision on these supplementary parameters makes the final result no less arbitrary, it does suggest the factors which were considered. Subsequent to the time the computations for the current investigation were performed, a study by Bailey (M. J. Bailey, "Capital Gains and Income Taxation," in A. C. Harberger and M. J. Bailey, eds., *The Taxation of Income From Capital,* Washington, D.C., The Brookings Institution, 1969, pp. 11–49) presented evidence suggesting that a number as low as 8 or 9 per cent would be a reasonable approximation of the actual effective tax rate on capital gains for the average investor. By that standard, the after-tax capital gains attributed here to executives—and, in consequence, the strength of the ownership-management income link—will tend to have been understated. Once again, therefore, the revision in the data which would be called for would only buttress the arguments made below.

indicated range. For consistency, 15 per cent was also designated as the effective tax rate on stock option profits in the compensation calculations. In both applications, capital gains and losses were treated symmetrically by imputing an associated 15 per cent tax *saving* to any declines in the market value of securities held, on the assumption that sufficient ultimate net profits would exist to provide a usable tax offset, should paper losses eventually emerge as realized losses.

The levies on executives' dividend receipts from holdings of their firms' shares present a slightly different problem. Given a progressive personal income tax schedule, the taxes assessed on such receipts, those on concurrent salary and bonus payments, and those on whatever additional income executives may enjoy from other sources, are interdependent. To ensure accuracy, the magnitude of each element for the relevant year for every individual should be specified prior to calculating the taxes on any one of the three. The difficulty is that in arriving at tax liabilities in connection with the original compensation study of large manufacturers, an estimate of the probable size of executives' total taxable noncompensation income (which would include inflows from investments in both their own *and* other companies' stock) had to be made.[20] As the dividend data, or at least that portion relating to ownership of employer-company shares, now become directly available, however, the initial outside income estimate of 15 per cent of a man's pre-tax annual salary plus bonus earnings begins to apear too low. Indeed, employer-company dividend payments to executives turn out to be sufficiently large in themselves as to suggest that a figure for total noncompensation income of approximately 30 per cent of the observed salary plus bonus payments would have been a better estimate to begin with.[21]

In the light of that evidence, the implication is that the compensation analysis should be repeated with an improved choice of parameters, and a new set of time series generated for the current investigation. Not surprisingly, that solution will be rejected here—but for reasons of principle as well as concern with the practical problem of

[20] See above, pp. 16–17.
[21] The data are presented in Chapter 4.

actually redoing the extensive calculations required. For one thing, the fact is that even if an underestimate of top management's aggregate taxable outside income has been made, the gain in accuracy which would be achieved by revising the estimate would be very small. Sensitivity tests with alternative assumptions about outside income ranging from zero to 50 per cent of salary plus bonus were undertaken as part of the original compensation study.[22] The clear conclusion was that the resulting historical profile of the components of the pay package for the typical executive would not have been significantly affected even by substantial changes in those assumptions.[23]

Secondly, a finding to the effect that executives' pre-tax dividend and interest income amounted on average to, say, 30 per cent as much as their pre-tax salary and bonus earnings would by no means imply that their total additional *taxable* income was of that magnitude. Just as the normal disposition of income received in the form of employee compensation gives rise to deductions for tax purposes, it is equally likely that the expenses associated with the maintenance of a large investment portfolio would cause the taxable income generated therefrom to be noticeably less than the corresponding gross income. In particular, it does not seem unreasonable to expect that fairly sizeable deductions for interest payments might frequently be claimed by executives as a consequence of having borrowed the funds to acquire some fraction of the equity portfolios we observe.[24] By that interpretation, the initial stipulation that effective tax rates on senior corporate officers' direct annual income could be calculated by assuming aggregate receipts equal to 115 per cent of recorded salary plus bonus payments does not, in retrospect, seem an inappropriate basis for the analysis. The tax liabilities on compensation prescribed by this assumption will, therefore, be retained here, and the relevant

[22] See the earlier discussion on p. 18.

[23] Lewellen, *op. cit.*, Chapter 12.

[24] The prevalence of this phenomenon was suggested to the author in conversations with V. Henry Rothschild II, whose book *Compensating the Corporate Executive* (New York, Ronald Press, Editions in 1942, 1951, and 1962), written in collaboration with G. T. Washington, is the classic work in the field of executive remuneration.

liabilities on the dividend income from holdings of employer-company shares will be determined simply by applying matching over-all effective tax rates to those payments as well.

To illustrate: An executive who was paid $100,000 in salary and bonus by his firm during a given year was specified, in the framework of the compensation investigation, to have enjoyed an additional $15,000 worth of current ordinary income from other sources. Let us suppose that, after the probable amounts of his deductions and exemptions were taken into consideration—by utilizing IRS data on income recipients in the $115,000 range for the year in question— the man's total personal tax liability was estimated to be $46,000. Of that aggregate figure, the fraction 100/115, or $40,000, would have been attributed to his salary and bonus payments, implying a 40 per cent over-all effective tax rate and an after-tax direct cash compensation of $60,000.

Accordingly, taxes at 40 per cent will be assumed here to apply to any dividend receipts enjoyed by the executive from ownership of his firm's shares—even if they turn out to exceed $15,000 before taxes for the relevant year. The same procedure will be followed for all three company samples examined, the compensation calculations in each case preceding the introduction of the attendant stock ownership data.

To the extent that the average executive's taxable income is thereby underestimated, the effect of these approximations will be an overstatement of after-tax salaries-plus-bonuses and after-tax dividend receipts, owing to an understatement of the pertinent tax liabilities.[25] This will, however, bias the findings in such a way as to make the relative importance of top management's ownership income depend-

[25] Some feeling for the degree of possible tax understatement which might be involved in a typical situation can be obtained from the example cited above. According to the federal personal income tax schedule that was in force from 1954 through 1963, the over-all effective tax rate on a gross income of $115,000 would have been 45.3 per cent, assuming deductions and exemptions at the general level indicated by IRS tabulations. The effective rate on $130,000—which might consist of $100,000 of salary and bonus plus an additional 30 per cent rather than 15 per cent outside income—would have been 47.4 per cent. That difference does not seem a cause for concern, even if it does actually denote an error.

ence appear *less* than it really is, since salaries and bonuses happen to comprise a larger share of total *compensation* than dividends comprise of total *ownership income*. If errors have been made by overoptimism about the magnitude of executives' deductions and exemptions from taxable income, then, the appropriate corrections would only strengthen the conclusions reached below. This issue will be addressed more precisely through sensitivity analyses as the data are developed.[26]

Net and Absolute Capital Gains

In connection with certain of the important comparisons, separate calculations will be presented for what are termed the "net" and "absolute" capital gains experienced by executives. The objective in so doing will be to go beyond the combined effects of annual corporate stock price changes on the wealth position of the entire group of men in the sample in order to highlight the *individual* profits and losses—whether realized or accrued—which comprise those aggregate figures. Thus, if it should occur that in a sample of 50 senior executives during a particular period, 25 enjoyed increases in the market value of their employer-company shareholdings amounting to $50,000 apiece, and the other 25 each suffered simultaneous $50,000 declines, it would follow that, on balance, no *net* capital gain was experienced by the group as a whole. On the other hand, it is also true that the mean *absolute* change in wealth for the 50 executives was fully $50,000 per capita. The choice as to which of these two measures of ownership income flows is the more relevant in a given situation is a function of the nature of the problem being examined. Still, it seems desirable that both be available for the researcher's—and the reader's—alternative interpretation. Conveniently enough, the stock prices of the various individual firms which were included in the three samples moved in similar directions with sufficient frequency that in most years the differences—except for sign—between the average net and absolute gains figures were slight.

[26] See, especially, Chapter 4.

The Large Manufacturing Sample

The group of corporations to whose executives' circumstances the foregoing analytical framework will be applied consists of 80 firms broken down into three distinct categories. As has been indicated, 50 of these firms are classed among the very largest of the nation's manufacturing enterprises,[27] and represent the sample which was compiled for the original study of executive compensation. They were chosen by a process which was designed to include literally the 50 largest such companies. However, problems with gaps in the necessary data, with mergers, and with the late stock exchange listings of certain firms prevented this goal from being achieved.

The basic reference source was *Fortune* magazine's roster of the five hundred largest industrials.[28] While corporations in that tabulation are ranked according to their sales volumes for the year, similar rankings by total assets, by profits, or by aggregate stock market values would result in essentially the same firms appearing on the corresponding lists.[29] The selection technique was simply to begin at the top and work down, including in the sample every company for whom sufficient information was available in past proxy statements to permit a meaningful historical analysis and evaluation of its top executives' remuneration. The description above, and in Appendix A, of the computational procedures employed suggests that the associated data requirements were reasonably stringent. As a consequence, the manner in which many firms chose to respond to the SEC's reporting rules for compensation made it impossible to include them in the investigation.

Similarly, because other companies of substantial size in 1963 had

[27] The combined sales of the 50 firms in 1963 were $93.8 billion, and total manufacturing sector revenues in that year were $417.3 billion. Source: United States Department of Commerce, *Survey of Current Business,* May 1965, p. S-4.

[28] "The Fortune Directory," *Fortune,* Vol. 70, No. 1 (July 1964), pp. 179–198.

[29] For example, when the corporations on the *Fortune* list were re-ranked on the basis of their total assets, only four of the initial top twenty in 1963 were not present among the top twenty on the revised list.

been formed by a series of mergers and acquisitions, the proxy statement records of their officers' pay did not always have enough consistency or continuity to allow a proper reconstruction of the relevant experience. Finally, even certain very large firms had been admitted to trading on an organized securities exchange—thereby coming under the disclosure regulations of the SEC—too recently to have generated an adequate public data history.[30]

For these reasons, it became necessary to reach down as far as the corporation which ranked 78th in sales volume in 1963 in order to round out a list of fifty concerns whose compensation policies could be traced with the requisite precision. Despite these minor difficulties, the resulting sample clearly encompasses a sufficiently broad range of industrial categories—some fifteen in all—and is comprised throughout of firms of sufficient size—sales running from $660 million to $16.5 billion in 1963—that the findings therefrom can appropriately be considered a fair representation of the scale and structure of managerial rewards in the nation's large, publicly held manufacturing enterprises. The complete list of firms involved is recorded in Appendix B.

The goal established was to collect data on as many executive positions in the corporate hierarchy as was feasible, and to go as far back in time as the proxy statement evidence would allow. Operationally, it turned out that the year 1940 was pretty well the practical limit of the analysis. The SEC first demanded formal proxy information of firms in the late 1930's, but the initial rules for reporting the compensation figures which are of interest here were not rigorous enough to bring about uniform and comprehensive disclosure for several years. With the exceptions noted above, however, it was possible to assemble a good history for most large companies from

---

[30] The SEC rules were tightened in the mid-1960's to require proxy statement compensation reports of many unlisted companies as well, but this change came too late to be of any help in connection with data for earlier periods. Perhaps the most prominent case of a large firm for which such information is unavailable is Ford Motor Company, whose shares were not listed on an exchange until 1956. A comparable problem still exists for Western Electric Company, which is one of the country's largest manufacturers but is a wholly owned subsidiary of AT&T and therefore not required to report its executives' earnings separately.

1940 on. The analysis ends with 1963 simply because that year was the latest for which data were available at the time the original study was begun.[31]

The number of individuals whose earnings and stockholdings are tabulated in the typical proxy statement varies widely from company to company—and, for that matter, very often from year to year within a given company. After a few trial runs, it became evident that in considering the entire group of firms, an evaluation of the remuneration and the ownership income associated with the *five* highest-paid executive positions in each would be the maximum coverage that the data would support with any reasonable consistency. A history of those five positions will therefore be the focus of the discussion. The sample that emerges includes 552 different individuals in the 50 corporations. Of the 6000 man-years of compensation and investment experience which would comprise a complete data matrix —i.e., five positions in 50 companies over 24 years—a total of roughly 5200 were filled in. A record of the resulting population, broken down by year and by executive rank, is presented in Appendix C.[32]

The Retail Trade Sample

As a counterpoint to that sample, information on a separate group of corporations engaged primarily in retail trade was compiled. While any one of a number of broad categories of firms could have provided a potentially interesting and useful contrast to the findings for the large industrials, retailers were chosen because they offered what seemed a sensible combination of characteristics for purposes of the study. The nature of their business activities differs markedly from that of manufacturers, thus allowing the structure of rewards in a

[31] The cooperation of the staff of the Baker Library at the Harvard Business School in securing access to the extensive collection of corporation records which that library maintains is gratefully acknowledged. Those documents provided the raw materials for both this investigation and its predecessor.

[32] This sample is marginally smaller than that which was included in the initial compensation study, since, as was indicated above, there were six executives for whom earnings data could be obtained but not stock ownership information.

substantially different organizational context to be examined. Convenient, up-to-date rankings of retailing enterprises by annual sales volume are furnished by *Fortune* magazine in the same way that the 500 largest industrials are tabulated each year. Since the common shares of most sizeable retailers have been listed and traded on securities exchanges for quite some time, good historical proxy statement data are available. Finally, the various elements of the executive compensation package have been developed by retail firms over the years to a degree that produces in the relevant earnings figures a rich background for an investigation of management's ownership income. If these attributes do not render retailers the *only* appropriate complementary sample choice, they do at least suggest a manifest suitability for the role.

The process of selecting particular companies paralleled that adopted in connection with the large manufacturing sample. Beginning at the top of the *Fortune* "Merchandising" rankings for 1963 and working downward,[33] the back proxy statement files of each successive firm were reviewed, and every corporation for which adequate historical information on executive remuneration and stockholdings could be assembled was included. In the interest of constructing as coherent a sample as possible, grocery chains were separated from the department-and-discount-store group, only the latter being considered. Logically, the decision could have gone either way, but the food retailers appeared to embody certain of the desirable characteristics noted above to a somewhat smaller extent than did their nonfood brethren. Consequently, they seemed a marginally less attractive choice. The 1963 *Fortune* list was employed simply to ensure maximum comparability of the findings with the original large manufacturing output. By the same reasoning, information was collected again for the period 1940 through 1963.

In all, a proper chronological analysis was feasible for the experience of the men who filled the top five executive positions at fifteen major retailers over the indicated period. The group encompasses fifteen of the first twenty-three on the *Fortune* roster—grocers and

[33] "The Fortune Directory: Part II," *Fortune,* Vol. LXX, No. 2 (August 1964), pp. 151–162.

wholesalers excluded—and it covers almost every important nation-wide or regional chain of department stores currently doing business. By way of comparison with the industrial sample, the companies at issue accounted in 1963 for $15.8 billion of the $246.4 billion aggregate United States retail sales.[34] Information on 192 different executives was gathered, and a resulting total of 1757 man-years of compensation history are involved.[35] Thus, in most dimensions, the sample is roughly one-fourth to one-third the size and relative importance of its large manufacturing counterpart. The specific firms included are listed in Appendix B, and the sample size each year by position can be found in Appendix C.

The Small Manufacturing Sample

The third group of enterprises studied consists of a collection of small manufacturers, the objective in their selection being an attempt to determine the degree to which the patterns of compensation and ownership income observed in large industrial corporations hold more generally for the manufacturing sector. Whether by some absolute standard the firms which ended up in the sample can fairly be termed "small" is perhaps a legitimate question, since the smallest among them had sales of $87 million, and the largest $139 million, in 1963. It is clear, however, that they operate in a much different market context and at a much more modest scale of activity than do the corresponding fifty large manufacturers. The difficulty with seeking a sample of still smaller companies is simply one of obtaining data. Complete past proxy statement records become considerably harder to put together—as well as significantly less informative in many instances—at the under-$100 million sales level. This occurs not only because of the later stock exchange listing of the majority of such firms, but also because their business and management history seems often to involve rather more in the way of periodic upheavals than the larger companies display. A corporation with $100 million

---

[34] Survey of Current Business, *op. cit.*, p. S-4.
[35] Out of the 1800—five positions in 15 companies for 24 years—which would constitute a full set.

sales in 1963 may, of course, have been a *very* small enterprise back in 1940, when the data we are interested in begin.[36]

The initial try at constructing the sample focused on the firms ranked 450th and below on the *Fortune* 1963 list, but of the resulting fifty-one possibilities, only four turned out in their proxy statements to provide enough consistent information on managerial earnings and stockholdings to permit the necessary analysis for their five highest-paid executive positions. The 400-to-449th category sub-sequently yielded another four, and it was not until the examination was extended to the companies ranked 350-to-399th that a group totaling fifteen, to at least match in size the retail trade sample, could be assembled.[37] Since the corporations included therein represent quite a broad range of industries, the decision was to stop at that point and to assume that the 196 executives and the 1,781 man-years of experience which emerged could be regarded as an adequate basis for drawing useful conclusions about the circumstances of the senior officers of smaller firms. Appendix B lists the relevant companies, and Appendix C tabulates, as before, the yearly sample size in each of the five positions.

Summary

An investigation of the ownership income enjoyed by professional managers seems an important undertaking because of its potential implications for both economic theory and economic practice. Not only do a great many of our normative models depend for their validity on the notion that the affairs of corporations are adminis-tered with the goal of profit maximization paramount in manage-ment's mind, but so do many of our consequent claims about the viability and vigor of the actual economy. The intention here is that the dimensions of the relationship between corporate performance and executive incomes be revealed in order that judgments about the possible effects of the prevailing separation of ownership and manage-

---

[36] Several of the firms eventually chosen, for example, had annual sales in the $6–$7 million range in the early 1940's.

[37] The largest firm was ranked 353rd in sales in 1963, and the smallest 495th.

ment may be arrived at in a more informed manner. The conceptual framework developed, and the attendant computational techniques, have been designed to cast up evidence that will foster such an understanding. They will be applied historically to three different samples, comprising a total of 80 companies, 940 executives, and approximately 8,750 man-years of income experience.

3

EXECUTIVE COMPENSATION PATTERNS

THE COMPENSATION which executives receive in return for their managerial efforts on behalf of the corporations which employ them forms the background to our appraisal of ownership income flows. The aggregate amounts of remuneration involved, the relative weight of each of the constituents, the changes observable over time, and the relationships among firms and between executive positions all merit our attention. It is only after these patterns of reward have been documented that the significance of management's dividend and capital gains experiences as shareholders can be put in perspective. The initial task, therefore, is to address the analytical procedures described in the preceding chapter to the earnings histories of the individual executives who make up the three samples with which we shall be concerned.

The Large Manufacturing Companies

Because the compensation of the senior officers of the fifty corporations in the large manufacturing sample has been examined in considerable detail in the original National Bureau volume cited, an abbreviated version of those findings should satisfy present requirements. We may begin by treating the chronology of the most familiar, as well as most easily obtainable, measure of executive pay: direct cash salary and bonus income. Table 1 records the mean values of such payments, both before and after taxes, from 1940 through 1963, for the top executive in each of the fifty firms and for the top five executives in each combined. The latter figures are calculated by adding the means determined for the five separate positions every year

TABLE 1

Average Salary Plus Bonus Earnings:
Large Manufacturing Sample, 1940–63
(amounts in dollars)

Year	Top Executive		Top Five Executives	
	Before Taxes	After Taxes	Before Taxes	After Taxes
1940	136,916	77,009	80,934	50,874
1941	143,138	66,437	85,101	44,018
1942	143,453	51,564	87,048	36,659
1943	144,208	43,036	88,054	31,886
1944	143,612	42,960	86,744	31,771
1945	142,892	42,818	87,066	31,815
1946	143,247	51,592	92,326	38,178
1947	149,446	53,051	94,596	38,843
1948	161,959	77,776	102,949	55,591
1949	169,703	80,270	108,134	57,427
1950	178,452	83,008	116,033	60,315
1951	182,876	79,396	122,592	59,474
1952	185,190	75,413	125,795	56,985
1953	193,556	77,717	133,459	59,382
1954	197,369	83,518	137,053	64,341
1955	205,121	85,508	143,257	66,171
1956	215,767	88,178	150,298	68,045
1957	207,586	86,303	146,248	67,248
1958	207,101	86,153	141,234	66,085
1959	205,741	86,369	144,423	67,234
1960	202,610	85,522	141,452	66,554
1961	200,375	85,057	137,855	65,313
1962	203,578	85,845	142,150	66,903
1963	212,230	88,095	150,264	69,526

and then dividing by five. In this instance, the rankings within the relevant firms are on the basis of salary plus bonus receipts alone, rather than according to the levels of *total* compensation enjoyed by the executives in question. The complete pay package, and its implied rankings, will be discussed below.[1]

From the tabulation, it is apparent that while the absolute amounts at issue are substantial, the rates of increase over the years are quite modest. The typical top executive received just 55 per cent more in the way of annual pre-tax direct current remuneration in 1963 than his predecessor did in 1940. For the top five men as a group, the gain was 86 per cent. Given that neither of these findings denote a really outstanding performance, the after-tax figures look even less impressive under the influence of a concomitant sharp rise in personal income tax rates.[2] Mean after-tax salaries and bonuses climbed by merely 14 and 37 per cent, respectively, for the top and top-five executive categories over the quarter-century interval shown. The lower-ranking men in the hierarchy did better historically both because their before-tax pay grew somewhat more rapidly, and because the burden of a progressive tax structure fell more lightly on their smaller absolute rewards.

When the after-tax "current income equivalents" of the same individuals' pension promises, deferred compensation, profit-sharing benefits, and stock options are added to the indicated salary and bonus earnings so as to arrive at the appropriate aggregate remuneration figures, the results listed in Table 2 and diagrammed in Chart 1 emerge. The ranking of executives within their firms here uses total after-tax compensation for the year as the ordering criterion. We see

[1] Most of the slight differences between certain of the figures presented here and those recorded in the original compensation study are attributable to the marginally smaller current sample size which resulted from the inability to secure stock ownership data for every year and for every man included in the earnings analysis (see Chapter 2). In addition, some minor improvements in the compensation data themselves were found to be possible on the second pass through the proxy statements.

[2] Only federal tax liabilities are taken into account in the analysis. The inclusion of state and local levies would, of course, reinforce the evidence that after-tax earnings have risen slowly.

TABLE 2

Average Total After-Tax Compensation:
Large Manufacturing Sample, 1940–63
(amounts in dollars)

Year	Top Executive	Top Five Executives
1940	101,979	59,673
1941	91,535	57,019
1942	65,960	44,545
1943	56,461	39,020
1944	63,667	41,720
1945	61,632	41,447
1946	69,043	47,919
1947	78,317	49,907
1948	99,754	67,427
1949	105,311	70,776
1950	122,790	78,995
1951	109,341	77,367
1952	116,657	79,551
1953	131,782	85,982
1954	143,470	93,267
1955	214,430	125,011
1956	235,674	136,365
1957	227,227	132,843
1958	168,807	108,945
1959	214,010	131,163
1960	224,853	133,464
1961	207,119	131,672
1962	228,232	139,245
1963	189,824	121,549
Average:		
1955–63	212,242	128,917

CHART I

AVERAGE TOTAL AFTER-TAX COMPENSATION: LARGE MANUFACTURING SAMPLE, 1940-63

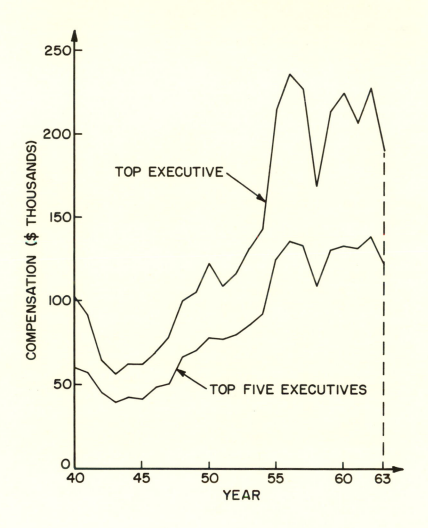

that, over time, the experience of the men in the sample appears a bit more favorable when this comprehensive view of the pay package is adopted. The annual after-tax rewards tabulated slightly better than doubled from 1940 to 1963 for both the top, and top-five, executive groups. The World War II declines—caused by heavy tax increases—were more than offset in the immediate postwar period; by the mid-1950's, significant gains in remuneration, as compared with prior years, were the rule.

One especially interesting feature of these data is the severe volatility of total executive income from year to year, likewise beginning in the mid-1950's. This is a direct consequence of the growing corporate reliance on forms of reward, such as stock options, in which shares of the employer company's common stock were utilized as the compensation medium. Fluctuations in the securities markets therefore came to be reflected strongly in managerial earnings, a phenomenon about which more will be said subsequently. In order to identify more clearly the levels which executive pay reached in the later years of the study, Chart 2 replicates the findings of Table 2, but with the annual after-tax remuneration provided by stock options during the years 1955 through 1963 spread evenly over that interval, and the revised total compensation figures replotted.[3] These smoothed data, because they highlight a kind of "plateau" in earnings which persisted generally for the last nine years depicted, will be extremely useful in several connections when one is drawing comparisons with executives' ownership income and with the other two company samples examined.

The secular shifts in emphasis within the pay package toward deferred and contingent items, and the volatility they introduced, are evident from Table 3, in which the components of aggregate remuneration are broken down for the two executive groups. The same data are diagrammed in Chart 3. Whereas, in the 1940's, salaries and bonuses accounted for roughly three-fourths of total pay for the top

[3] That is, the nine relevant option earnings figures for 1955–63 were added within each of the five executive positions, the five means obtained, and the results substituted for the original annual option figures at each rank.

CHART 2

AVERAGE TOTAL AFTER-TAX COMPENSATION: LARGE MANUFACTURING SAMPLE, 1940-63 (STOCK OPTION DATA SMOOTHED)

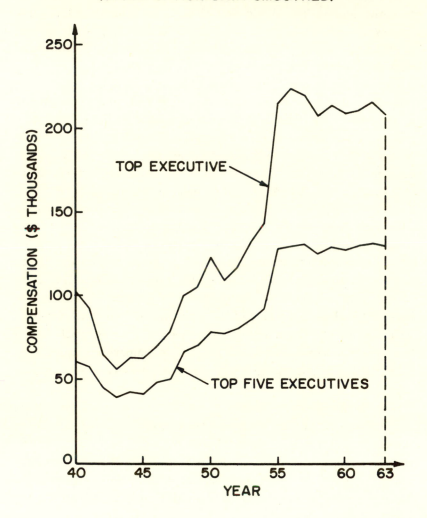

TABLE 3

Elements of After-Tax Compensation:
Large Manufacturing Sample, 1940–63
(amounts in dollars)

Year	Top Executive		Top Five Executives	
	Salary and Bonus	Noncurrent Rewards	Salary and Bonus	Noncurrent Rewards
1940	76,382 (75)	25,597 (25)	50,847 (85)	8,826 (15)
1941	65,804 (72)	25,731 (28)	43,869 (77)	13,150 (23)
1942	49,627 (75)	16,333 (25)	36,445 (82)	8,100 (18)
1943	42,523 (75)	13,938 (25)	31,625 (81)	7,395 (19)
1944	41,795 (66)	21,872 (34)	31,493 (75)	10,227 (25)
1945	41,221 (67)	20,411 (33)	31,676 (76)	9,771 (24)
1946	48,569 (70)	20,474 (30)	38,072 (79)	9,847 (21)
1947	51,497 (66)	26,820 (34)	38,800 (78)	11,107 (22)
1948	75,201 (75)	24,553 (25)	55,536 (82)	11,891 (18)
1949	78,767 (75)	26,544 (25)	57,334 (81)	13,442 (19)
1950	79,595 (65)	43,195 (35)	60,183 (76)	18,812 (24)
1951	74,536 (68)	34,805 (32)	59,167 (76)	18,200 (24)
1952	71,894 (62)	44,763 (38)	56,893 (72)	22,658 (28)
1953	73,100 (55)	58,682 (45)	59,195 (69)	26,787 (31)
1954	78,353 (55)	65,117 (45)	64,243 (69)	29,024 (31)
1955	79,480 (37)	134,950 (63)	66,036 (53)	58,975 (47)
1956	81,347 (35)	154,327 (65)	68,009 (50)	68,356 (50)
1957	80,736 (36)	146,491 (64)	67,566 (51)	65,277 (49)
1958	80,985 (48)	87,822 (52)	65,894 (60)	43,051 (40)
1959	82,695 (39)	131,315 (61)	67,022 (51)	64,141 (49)
1960	80,733 (36)	144,120 (64)	66,056 (49)	67,408 (51)
1961	80,741 (39)	126,378 (61)	65,369 (50)	66,303 (50)
1962	79,539 (35)	148,693 (65)	67,207 (48)	72,038 (52)
1963	83,568 (44)	106,256 (56)	68,982 (57)	52,567 (43)
Averages:				
1940–49	57,139 (72)	22,227 (28)	41,570 (80)	10,376 (20)
1955–63	81,092 (38)	131,150 (62)	66,905 (52)	62,012 (48)

NOTE: Numbers in parentheses denote per cent of after-tax total each year.

CHART 3

ELEMENTS OF TOTAL AFTER-TAX COMPENSATION:
LARGE MANUFACTURING SAMPLE, 1940-63

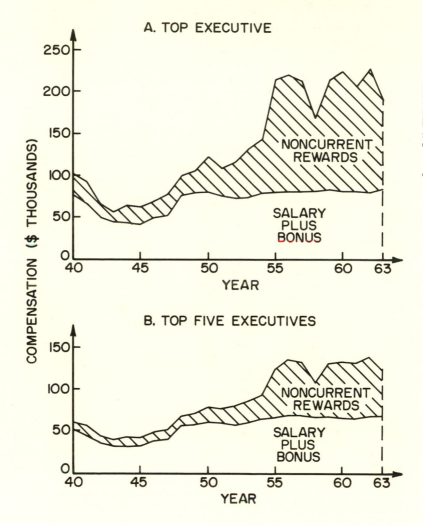

men in each firm, that contribution had dropped to just a little more than one-third by the late 1950's and early 1960's. For the top five men together, the corresponding change was from four-fifths down to one-half of the total.[4] Thus, direct cash compensation subject to immediate taxation has not merely declined in relative importance over the years, but has, in a great many instances, actually fallen to a minority role in the over-all structure of rewards.[5] The significance of this development can perhaps best be appreciated when we observe that virtually all of the recorded growth in the earnings of the senior management group in large manufacturing enterprises between 1940 and 1963 can be traced to the introduction and expanded utilization of deferred and contingent arrangements. Had salaries and bonuses remained the dominant source of executive income, the men in the sample would very likely have been little better off in the 1960's than they were before World War II.

Even with the emergence of noncash forms of compensation, however, the historical earnings experience of these executives still turns out to be relatively poor in comparison with other changes that have taken place in the environment since 1940. The companies for whom the men worked—and, presumably, whose success depended on the policies they formulated—have grown much more rapidly in every important dimension. The income of other professional occupational groups increased at a noticeably faster pace, as did the remuneration of individuals at the lower end of the corporate organizational structure—manufacturing production workers. In fact, the price level in the community rose between 1940 and 1963 at almost exactly the same rate as total after-tax managerial pay, implying that no advances at all in real income terms were achieved by the indicated senior executives during the quarter-century at issue. The following tabulation summarizes the comparisons:

[4] The annual amounts tabulated for items other than salary and bonus represent, of course, the sum of their after-tax current income equivalents as defined in Chapter 2. All are mean values for the sample.

[5] The salary-plus-bonus figures in Table 3 differ somewhat from those in Table 1 because, as noted, the executive rankings are now established according to the levels of *aggregate* after-tax remuneration calculated.

COMPOUND ANNUAL RATES OF GROWTH, 1940–63

A. The 50 Sample Companies (aggregate figures):

Assets	7.0%
Net Worth	6.8
Sales	9.1
Profits, Before Taxes	9.1
Profits, After Taxes	8.1
Equity Market Value	10.2

B. After-Tax Earnings, Other Occupations:

Physicians	5.2%
Lawyers	3.9
Dentists	5.2
Manufacturing Production Workers	5.5

C. Consumer Price Index   3.4%

D. Total After-Tax Manufacturing Executive Compensation:

Top Executives	3.2%
Top Five Executives	3.3

The rates of growth in executive pay listed are computed by using as the values for 1963 the annual compensation averages over the period 1955–63 for each of the two categories (see Table 2). The fluctuations in yearly earnings noted above suggest that such averages are more reliable indices of attained levels of remuneration than the figure for any single recent year would be.[6] While evidence of this sort alone does not, of course, permit the inference that senior industrial executives have come to be underpaid as compared with a rigorous measure of their worth to their firms—their respective marginal revenue products—it *is* clear that a realignment of earnings relationships has occurred within the interval examined.[7]

---

[6] The corresponding figures for the professions and for hourly workers do not exhibit similar annual fluctuations. The data on sample-company characteristics, professional incomes, production workers' wages, and price changes are drawn from the original compensation study (Lewellen, *op. cit.,* Chapter 9). The equity market value data represent high-low price averages for each year.

[7] The difference between, say, a 3 per cent and a 6 per cent compound annual growth rate over twenty-three years, it should be pointed out, is the

Identification of the most significant characteristic of aggregate executive compensation for our present purposes, however, requires a different perspective on the data presented. If our concern is primarily with the possible links between managerial and shareholder incomes, the importance of common-stock-based sources of reward in the totals heretofore recorded is of special interest. That issue is addressed in Table 4 for the top, and top-five, executive groups, and the findings are depicted in Chart 4. Included in the category "stock-based" in the tabulations are stock options, stock bonuses, and any deferred compensation or profit-sharing plans in which the amounts set aside for the participants are invested in—and later distributed in the form of—shares of the employer corporation's common stock. Arrangements such as salaries and cash bonuses, pensions and cash deferred pay, and profit-sharing schemes are denoted "fixed dollar" rewards. For situations wherein a portion of the relevant benefits under a given plan were payable in cash and the remainder in stock, separate figures for each segment were compiled and allocated to the appropriate columns. Insofar as the magnitude and timing of certain of the fixed-dollar payments themselves were determined by firms as a function of, say, annual gross profits, the comparisons offered here will, of course, understate the true extent of management's effective earnings dependence on company performance.

As they stand, the data show that the highest-paid individuals in these 50 large manufacturing corporations received, on average, just under *half* their aggregate after-tax remuneration from stock-based devices of one kind or another during the period 1955 through 1963. For the five highest-paid executives in each firm combined, the proportion was one-third of total pay.[8] In both instances, these contributions represent increases from figures which were in the neighborhood of 2 to 5 per cent of earnings in the early 1940's. The growing volatility of senior executives' annual compensation in recent years appears as a direct result.

difference between a doubling and a quadrupling of the initial value. Fairly small variations in the annual percentages therefore give rise to substantial disparities in the over-all results.

[8] The criteria throughout being the magnitude of the various "after-tax current income equivalents" of the noncurrent rewards in question.

TABLE 4

Components of Total After-Tax Compensation:
Large Manufacturing Sample, 1940–63
(amounts in dollars)

	Top Executive		Top Five Executives	
Year	Earnings from Fixed-Dollar Rewards	Earnings from Stock-Based Rewards	Earnings from Fixed-Dollar Rewards	Earnings from Stock-Based Rewards
1940	98,755 (97)	3,224 (3)	56,904 (95)	2,769 (5)
1941	88,776 (97)	2,759 (3)	54,757 (96)	2,262 (4)
1942	63,864 (97)	2,096 (3)	42,787 (96)	1,759 (4)
1943	54,467 (97)	1,994 (3)	37,486 (96)	1,534 (4)
1944	62,353 (98)	1,314 (2)	40,787 (98)	933 (2)
1945	60,682 (98)	950 (2)	40,780 (98)	667 (2)
1946	68,295 (99)	748 (1)	46,974 (98)	945 (2)
1947	77,693 (99)	624 (1)	49,306 (99)	601 (1)
1948	97,379 (98)	2,375 (2)	66,028 (98)	1,400 (2)
1949	99,450 (94)	5,861 (6)	68,202 (96)	2,575 (4)
1950	113,944 (93)	8,846 (7)	75,146 (95)	3,849 (5)
1951	99,317 (91)	10,024 (9)	72,843 (94)	4,524 (6)
1952	96,563 (83)	20,094 (17)	70,791 (89)	8,760 (11)
1953	102,072 (77)	29,710 (23)	74,242 (86)	11,740 (14)
1954	110,582 (77)	32,888 (23)	80,811 (87)	12,456 (13)
1955	130,450 (61)	83,980 (39)	90,332 (72)	34,679 (28)
1956	125,208 (53)	110,466 (47)	89,153 (65)	47,212 (35)
1957	127,552 (56)	99,675 (44)	90,023 (68)	42,820 (32)
1958	115,935 (69)	52,872 (31)	84,322 (77)	24,623 (23)
1959	121,837 (57)	92,173 (43)	85,779 (65)	45,383 (35)
1960	116,445 (52)	108,408 (48)	83,727 (63)	49,737 (37)
1961	111,100 (54)	96,019 (46)	81,657 (62)	50,015 (38)
1962	115,906 (51)	112,326 (49)	85,854 (62)	53,390 (38)
1963	107,596 (57)	82,228 (43)	84,357 (69)	37,191 (31)
Average 1955–63	119,115 (56)	93,127 (44)	86,134 (67)	42,783 (33)

NOTE: Numbers in parentheses denote per cent of total each year.

CHART 4

COMPONENTS OF TOTAL AFTER-TAX COMPENSATION: LARGE MANUFACTURING SAMPLE, 1940-63

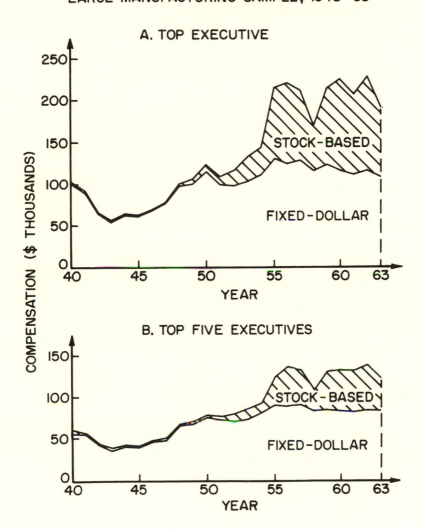

A. TOP EXECUTIVE

B. TOP FIVE EXECUTIVES

That volatility turns out to be greater, the higher in the managerial hierarchy a man climbs, since the emphasis on stock-based arrangements in his pay package rises simultaneously. Thus, a breakdown of the data by position indicates the following:

SOURCES OF AFTER-TAX COMPENSATION, 1955–63

Executive Rank	Per Cent of Total Earnings	
	Fixed-Dollar	Stock-Based
#1	56%	44%
#2	66	34
#3	69	31
#4	77	23
#5	81	19

On the basis of these findings alone, we might be tempted to conclude that executives' fortunes have become tied sufficiently strongly to their shareholders' economic interests over the years that nowadays a professional manager would be unlikely to adopt policies inimical to those interests. If nothing else, the evidence is at least consistent with the notion of such a general congruence of goals, and it establishes the existence of a relationship whose dimensions have not previously been well-documented. In that light, it comprises an important part of the story which the data on stock ownership below will complete.[9]

The Retail Trade Sample

The senior executives of the 15 large retailing firms examined display a historical compensation experience which, in its broad outlines, is similar to that of their manufacturing counterparts. In particular, the rates of growth in earnings observed since 1940 are

---

[9] It should be stressed again that none of the foregoing figures include any dividends or capital gains resulting from actual outright ownership of employer-company shares by executives. That "investment" income is recorded—as it will be in subsequent chapters—only *after* the relevant shares are formally conveyed to the executive and are valued here first as compensation receipts. See the discussion in Chapter 2.

roughly comparable, and the same trend toward heavier emphasis on deferred and contingent devices can again be seen. In this respect, the findings for the large manufacturers—and the implications thereof —are confirmed more generally for the managerial community. On the other hand, the differences in the results for the two samples are equally noteworthy. These relate primarily to the nature of the hierarchical compensation profile within companies, and they allow some interesting contrasts to be drawn.

The mean salary plus bonus income of the top, and top-five, officer categories in retailing is listed for the years 1940 to 1963 in Table 5.[10] While the absolute values shown are approximately two-thirds to three-fourths the size of the manufacturing averages throughout, the proportionate increases over time match up well with those indicated in Table 1. The highest-salaried men in each retailing firm enjoyed a 55 per cent gain in mean before-tax annual direct cash receipts; and the five highest-salaried together, a 63 per cent gain, between the beginning and the end of the interval studied. These compare with figures of 55 and 86 per cent, respectively, for the fifty large manufacturers.

Because increases of this order are fairly modest for a quarter-century of activity—and because personal tax rates were raised concurrently—the after-tax record is again unimposing. The corresponding take-home amounts for retail executives appreciated by just 19 and 26 per cent at the two levels in question. Clearly, those findings would suggest a pronounced upward rigidity in corporate pay policies at the top of the organizational structure.

The aggregate remuneration experience, however, belies such a ready interpretation. As Table 6 and Chart 5 illustrate, the mean total after-tax compensation of senior retailing executives somewhat more than doubled from 1940 to 1963. The figures were computed by adding to after-tax salary plus bonus receipts the after-tax current income equivalents of all other rewards observed, and then reranking individuals within their companies according to the new totals. From this standpoint, both the top, and top-five, executive groups display an income history which is a near-duplicate of the large-manufacturing data. While a "plateau" in earnings in the present instance does

[10] The rankings there are by salary plus bonus payments only.

TABLE 5

Average Salary Plus Bonus Earnings:
Retail Trade Sample, 1940–63
(amounts in dollars)

Year	Top Executive		Top Five Executives	
	Before Taxes	After Taxes	Before Taxes	After Taxes
1940	93,382	58,666	65,926	44,833
1941	113,405	55,995	76,487	41,151
1942	109,643	43,661	77,868	34,764
1943	111,859	37,602	79,259	30,861
1944	115,674	38,292	82,601	31,595
1945	112,567	37,833	82,552	31,661
1946	133,816	49,535	95,685	39,663
1947	122,131	46,878	96,153	39,981
1948	123,272	65,366	96,722	54,427
1949	117,094	63,060	90,586	51,940
1950	122,272	65,098	97,486	54,879
1951	116,057	59,835	91,376	50,463
1952	115,873	55,928	89,262	46,361
1953	118,993	57,005	91,115	46,985
1954	120,186	61,369	93,242	51,091
1955	135,299	65,938	99,865	53,420
1956	136,026	66,048	100,404	53,609
1957	135,622	66,098	100,704	53,847
1958	132,849	65,258	101,470	54,268
1959	142,299	68,082	106,336	55,907
1960	135,294	66,199	102,679	54,777
1961	141,627	68,293	104,488	55,377
1962	143,137	68,834	105,844	55,963
1963	144,452	69,606	107,623	56,704

TABLE 6

Average Total After-Tax Compensation:
Retail Trade Sample, 1940–63
(amounts in dollars)

Year	Top Executive	Top Five Executives
1940	59,148	45,304
1941	57,338	41,769
1942	48,602	37,497
1943	49,709	36,884
1944	56,976	38,450
1945	44,404	35,762
1946	62,757	45,462
1947	59,730	45,586
1948	79,776	60,865
1949	95,043	66,004
1950	75,662	61,580
1951	71,793	58,126
1952	68,652	55,406
1953	70,410	56,321
1954	96,039	67,933
1955	90,580	68,778
1956	98,324	71,740
1957	109,314	78,834
1958	117,514	81,629
1959	128,091	88,684
1960	116,513	84,694
1961	136,617	94,227
1962	133,456	92,277
1963	127,290	95,180
Average: 1959–63	128,393	91,012

CHART 5

AVERAGE TOTAL AFTER-TAX COMPENSATION: RETAIL TRADE SAMPLE, 1940-63

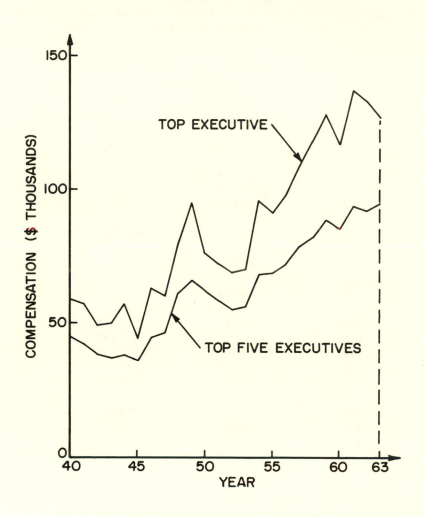

not appear to occur until perhaps 1959, rather than as early as 1955, the over-all record of pay increases is remarkably like that identified earlier for industrial firms. Presumably, a similar set of market forces and environmental pressures were at work.

The more vigorous performance of total compensation over the years vis-à-vis salaries and bonuses is, of course, attributable to the same growing reliance on noncurrent forms of remuneration to which the manufacturing time series attested. The retail sector does, on the other hand, exhibit this phenomenon to a smaller degree. Table 7 and Chart 6 show that the highest-paid executives in large retailing organizations received approximately *half* their earnings from arrangements other than salary and bonus during the last few years investigated.[11] For the large-manufacturing sample, the corresponding proportion was roughly two-thirds. In like fashion, the five highest-paid retail officers combined relied on noncurrent rewards for 39 per cent of their total after-tax pay in the early 1960's, as compared with a figure of 48 per cent in the case of their industrial counterparts. Nonetheless, because the pre-World War II percentages tabulated for both retail officer groups were quite small, a sharp secular restructuring of the compensation package is again evident.

One consequence of the more important role for salaries and bonuses—which are characteristically among the more stable income elements—in retail executives' earnings is a somewhat less volatile behavior of total annual remuneration than was indicated by the manufacturing analysis. The peaks and troughs recorded in Table 6 are not nearly as prominent in recent years as those depicted in Table 2. We shall examine this difference further in a subsequent comparison.

The fact that, despite these variations in experience, historical aggregate compensation growth rates in retailing and manufacturing have been very similar implies that the senior retail management group has also lost ground over time in relation to the pay of other professional occupations and has just about held its own in terms of purchasing power. In addition, the retail firms themselves expanded

[11] The differences between these salary-plus-bonus figures and those in Table 5 are attributable to the reranking of individuals within firms now by total compensation rather than by cash payments alone.

TABLE 7

Elements of After-Tax Compensation:
Retail Trade Sample, 1940–63
(amounts in dollars)

Year	Top Executive		Top Five Executives	
	Salary and Bonus	Noncurrent Rewards	Salary and Bonus	Noncurrent Rewards
1940	58,666 (99)	482 (1)	44,835 (99)	469 (1)
1941	55,995 (98)	1,343 (2)	41,120 (98)	648 (2)
1942	43,661 (90)	4,941 (10)	34,752 (93)	2,745 (7)
1943	36,904 (74)	12,805 (26)	30,855 (84)	6,029 (16)
1944	37,278 (65)	19,698 (35)	31,652 (82)	6,799 (18)
1945	36,259 (82)	8,145 (18)	31,582 (88)	4,180 (12)
1946	49,068 (78)	13,689 (22)	39,663 (87)	5,799 (13)
1947	45,941 (77)	13,789 (23)	39,994 (88)	5,591 (12)
1948	63,500 (80)	16,276 (20)	54,387 (89)	6,478 (11)
1949	60,288 (63)	34,755 (37)	51,741 (78)	14,263 (22)
1950	62,744 (83)	12,918 (17)	54,769 (89)	6,811 (11)
1951	57,872 (81)	13,921 (19)	50,527 (87)	7,599 (13)
1952	54,074 (79)	14,578 (21)	46,350 (84)	9,056 (16)
1953	54,834 (78)	15,576 (22)	46,920 (83)	9,401 (17)
1954	57,524 (60)	38,515 (40)	50,975 (75)	16,958 (25)
1955	65,683 (73)	24,897 (27)	53,373 (78)	15,406 (22)
1956	64,185 (65)	34,139 (35)	53,398 (74)	18,342 (26)
1957	65,824 (60)	43,490 (40)	53,716 (68)	25,119 (32)
1958	64,295 (55)	53,219 (45)	54,039 (66)	27,590 (34)
1959	64,283 (50)	63,808 (50)	55,405 (62)	33,279 (38)
1960	63,120 (54)	53,393 (46)	54,275 (64)	30,419 (36)
1961	66,657 (49)	69,960 (51)	55,264 (59)	38,964 (41)
1962	63,461 (48)	69,995 (52)	55,945 (61)	36,332 (39)
1963	66,833 (53)	60,457 (47)	56,590 (59)	38,590 (41)
Average: 1959–63	64,871 (51)	63,522 (49)	55,496 (61)	35,516 (39)

NOTE: Numbers in parentheses denote per cent of after-tax total each year.

CHART 6

ELEMENTS OF TOTAL AFTER-TAX COMPENSATION: RETAIL TRADE SAMPLE, 1940-63

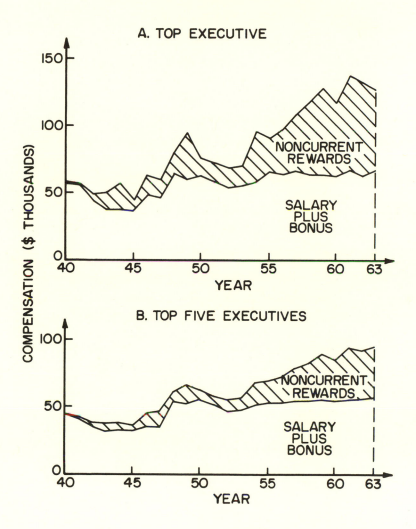

A. TOP EXECUTIVE

B. TOP FIVE EXECUTIVES

more rapidly by every significant measure than did the remuneration of their top officials, a result which again resembles the manufacturing findings. For example:

COMPOUND ANNUAL RATES OF GROWTH, 1940–63

A. The 15 Retailing Companies (Aggregate Figures):

Assets	7.2%
Sales	7.3
Profits, Before Taxes	7.1
Profits, After Taxes	5.8
Equity Market Values	7.8

B. Total After-Tax Retail Executive Compensation: [12]

Top Executives	3.4%
Top Five Executives	3.0

The generally sluggish chronological record of executive rewards therefore appears to extend beyond the circumstances of the industrial sector.

The intra-firm structure of rewards in retailing, however, has its own set of parameters. Specifically, the compensation spread among the men at the top of the several organizations is considerably narrower than is true of manufacturing enterprises. Thus:

BEFORE-TAX SALARY-PLUS-BONUS AS A PER CENT OF
TOP EXECUTIVE'S SALARY-PLUS-BONUS

Executive Rank *	Retail Trade		Manufacturing	
	1940–41	1959–63	1940–41	1955–63
#1	100%	100%	100%	100%
#2	73	79	63	75
#3	61	69	50	64
#4	57	63	45	57
#5	53	61	38	53

* By salary and bonus receipts.

[12] Based in this case on the 1959–63 compensation averages as the assumed terminal values for the 23-year interval at issue. See the commentary on page 48.

The two different averaging periods adopted for the two samples in the later years examined are functions simply of the times at which some coherent pattern in both the level and the composition of earnings seemed to evolve in the two instances. Alternative choices would yield equivalent comparisons, since the phenomenon identified is a persistent one. More important, it shows up in the total compensation figures as well:

TOTAL AFTER-TAX COMPENSATION AS A PER CENT OF
TOP EXECUTIVE'S TOTAL AFTER-TAX COMPENSATION

Executive Rank *	Retail Trade		Manufacturing	
	1940–41	1959–63	1940–41	1955–63
#1	100%	100%	100%	100%
#2	79	77	65	67
#3	69	65	53	55
#4	65	57	45	44
#5	61	55	39	38

* By total compensation.

Whatever our index, then, the remuneration gradient at the senior executive level is clearly much gentler for retailers. A full appraisal of these findings and their implications, on the other hand, exceeds the legitimate needs of the current study and can be better dealt with elsewhere.[13]

The key item in the present context is the proportion of total executive pay which is accounted for by stock-related forms of reward. Table 8 and Chart 7 show that the highest-paid men in the 15 firms received 1 per cent or less of their aggregate earnings from such devices in the early 1940's, but experienced 35 per cent of a sub-

[13] One possible explanation for the smaller retail pay differentials is the chain-store nature of the typical organization. Many of the corporate vice presidents in retailing appear to hold their positions by virtue of being the chief operating officers of one of the major stores in the chain, for which the parent organization is a kind of holding company. In manufacturing, by contrast, there is usually a functional-area division of responsibilities at the vice presidential level.

TABLE 8

Components of Total After-Tax Compensation:
Retail Trade Sample, 1940–63
(amounts in dollars)

	Top Executive		Top Five Executives	
Year	Earnings from Fixed-Dollar Rewards	Earnings from Stock-Based Rewards	Earnings from Fixed-Dollar Rewards	Earnings from Stock-Based Rewards
1940	58,718 (99)	430 (1)	45,080 (100)	223 (0)
1941	56,587 (99)	751 (1)	41,510 (99)	258 (1)
1942	48,409 (100)	193 (0)	37,407 (100)	89 (0)
1943	49,557 (100)	152 (0)	36,708 (100)	175 (0)
1944	55,803 (98)	1,173 (2)	38,041 (99)	409 (1)
1945	43,239 (97)	1,165 (3)	35,248 (99)	513 (1)
1946	57,842 (92)	4,915 (8)	44,099 (97)	1,362 (3)
1947	59,424 (99)	306 (1)	45,430 (100)	154 (0)
1948	78,247 (98)	1,529 (2)	60,329 (99)	535 (1)
1949	94,550 (99)	493 (1)	65,675 (100)	328 (0)
1950	74,482 (98)	1,180 (2)	60,994 (99)	585 (1)
1951	70,892 (99)	901 (1)	57,582 (99)	543 (1)
1952	67,434 (98)	1,218 (2)	54,628 (99)	777 (1)
1953	68,688 (98)	1,722 (2)	55,213 (98)	1,108 (2)
1954	91,791 (96)	4,248 (4)	65,232 (96)	2,700 (4)
1955	80,049 (88)	10,531 (12)	61,905 (90)	6,873 (10)
1956	87,584 (89)	10,740 (11)	64,678 (90)	7,061 (10)
1957	94,292 (86)	15,022 (14)	69,822 (89)	9,011 (11)
1958	91,683 (78)	25,831 (22)	67,384 (83)	14,244 (17)
1959	89,253 (70)	38,838 (30)	67,724 (76)	20,959 (24)
1960	81,194 (70)	35,319 (30)	65,752 (78)	18,941 (22)
1961	79,338 (58)	57,279 (42)	65,599 (70)	28,628 (30)
1962	80,726 (60)	52,730 (40)	67,520 (73)	24,756 (27)
1963	87,222 (69)	40,068 (31)	69,346 (73)	25,833 (27)
Average: 1959–63	83,547 (65)	44,846 (35)	67,188 (74)	23,824 (26)

NOTE: Numbers in parentheses denote per cent of total each year.

CHART 7

COMPONENTS OF TOTAL AFTER-TAX COMPENSATION:
RETAIL TRADE SAMPLE, 1940 - 63

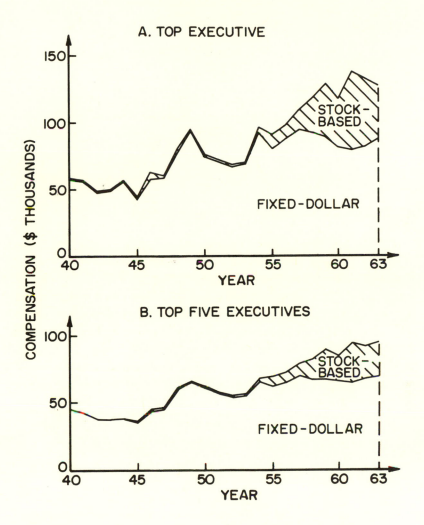

A. TOP EXECUTIVE

B. TOP FIVE EXECUTIVES

stantially higher total from the same sources between 1959 and 1963. The five highest-paid men, taken together, started from a comparably low base to end up with a 26 per cent contribution in the later years. The breakdown by position is as follows:

SOURCES OF AFTER-TAX RETAIL EXECUTIVE
COMPENSATION, 1959–63

Executive Rank *	Per Cent of Total Earnings	
	Fixed-Dollar	Stock-Based
#1	65%	35%
#2	73	27
#3	76	24
#4	80	20
#5	81	19

* By total compensation.

These are far from trivial fractions and are only slightly below the corresponding stock percentages for the large manufacturing sample. The fact that they *are* slightly below explains in part the somewhat less pronounced volatility of annual after-tax pay in retailing than in manufacturing.[14] Nonetheless, the phenomenon of an important direct link between managerial compensation and shareholder returns appears to hold for the leading firms in this sector of the economy as well, even though separation of ownership and management would, in the usual view, be alleged a potential problem in their operations because of the wide public stock distribution that they enjoy.

The Small Manufacturing Sample

The compensation history associated with the senior executive positions in smaller industrial enterprises provides additional support for

[14] As it happens, the bulk of retail executives' stock-based earnings originate in post-retirement deferred compensation plans, while stock options are the dominant element in manufacturing. Since the former generally give rise to milder annual fluctuations in value in response to a particular change in stock prices due to the longer planning and accrual horizon involved, it is consistent to observe a greater degree of income stability in the retail remuneration figures.

the central conclusions which the foregoing data suggest.[15] There is an especially strong resemblance between the structure and the chronology of managerial earnings in such companies and those of executives in very large manufacturing corporations. Indeed, the similarity both in rates of growth of total pay and in intra-firm compensation differentials for the two samples is sufficiently marked as to imply that they are symptomatic of some basic attributes of industrial organizations in this country.

The record of salary-plus-bonus payments to the senior officers of the 15 companies which comprise the small-firm sample is presented in Table 9. We see that the mean pre-tax direct cash remuneration of the highest-salaried men in each firm increased by 67 per cent between 1940 and 1963, while that of the five highest-salaried, as a group, rose by 108 per cent. This is a more impressive performance than that displayed by the corresponding large-manufacturing time series. It does, however, fit logically and neatly into a consistent overall result, whose dimensions we shall examine.

The attendant after-tax magnitudes—calculated according to the procedures regarding outside income, deductions, and exemptions described in Chapter 2—were 31 per cent greater in 1963 than in 1940 for the typical top executive. For the top five men combined, the gain was 58 per cent. Because the *absolute* pre-tax amounts involved are substantially below those enjoyed by the large-manufacturing managerial contingent, progressive personal income taxes fall rather more lightly over the years on the current sample, raising the proportion of take-home pay to gross receipts throughout, as well as enhancing the observed historical growth rates in the after-tax figures.

The secular pattern of *total* after-tax compensation experienced by small-manufacturing executives is recorded in Table 10 and illustrated by Chart 8. These data indicate that during the quarter-century interval studied, mean aggregate annual remuneration almost exactly doubled, both for the highest-paid, and for the five highest-paid, individuals in each company. Average earnings for the period 1956–63 are utilized in making that comparison—once again simply as a

---

[15] It should be noted again that "smaller" refers here to firms with annual sales in the $100 million range. See Chapter 2.

TABLE 9

Average Salary Plus Bonus Earnings:
Small Manufacturing Sample, 1940–63
(amounts in dollars)

| | Top Executive | | Top Five Executives | |
| | --- | --- | --- | --- |
Year	Before Taxes	After Taxes	Before Taxes	After Taxes
1940	51,598	37,264	30,353	24,207
1941	53,916	31,744	32,621	21,555
1942	55,274	27,996	33,907	19,693
1943	53,339	24,329	32,547	17,449
1944	54,584	24,666	33,029	17,636
1945	55,487	24,896	34,055	18,047
1946	58,829	29,047	37,883	21,247
1947	62,526	30,202	41,419	22,707
1948	66,559	41,114	42,981	29,116
1949	63,494	40,106	41,847	28,733
1950	68,576	42,722	42,906	29,302
1951	70,333	42,216	46,509	30,550
1952	76,692	42,002	49,210	30,013
1953	76,819	42,132	48,516	29,755
1954	75,181	44,128	47,966	31,136
1955	76,792	44,772	50,094	32,221
1956	84,103	47,851	53,488	33,849
1957	84,279	47,894	53,611	33,946
1958	81,466	46,594	52,953	33,638
1959	88,362	49,518	57,635	35,760
1960	84,567	48,033	58,397	36,256
1961	82,575	47,135	57,763	35,876
1962	85,971	48,609	61,603	37,538
1963	86,071	48,607	63,044	38,201

TABLE 10

Average Total After-Tax Compensation:
Small Manufacturing Sample, 1940–63
(amounts in dollars)

Year	Top Executive	Top Five Executives
1940	37,682	24,502
1941	33,201	22,088
1942	29,481	20,227
1943	26,591	18,031
1944	28,001	18,991
1945	26,870	19,617
1946	30,877	22,886
1947	38,616	27,162
1948	46,595	32,607
1949	56,915	34,607
1950	51,872	33,728
1951	49,361	34,588
1952	49,360	34,106
1953	60,351	38,324
1954	65,472	40,224
1955	64,244	41,854
1956	85,126	49,735
1957	77,648	46,262
1958	69,513	44,457
1959	66,889	47,916
1960	70,165	51,252
1961	66,422	49,093
1962	94,486	57,459
1963	65,550	48,414
Average: 1956–63	74,475	49,324

CHART 8

AVERAGE TOTAL AFTER-TAX COMPENSATION: SMALL MANUFACTURING SAMPLE, 1940-63

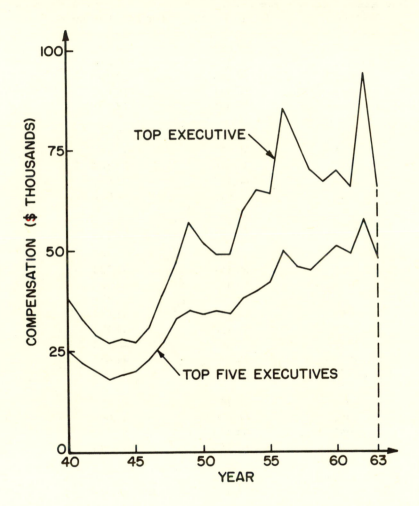

device to circumvent the recent volatility in the yearly figures. On this basis, the full compensation history of senior management in small industrial firms comes extremely close to that exhibited by the two previous samples. Clearly, the conclusion that such a result may be interpreted as evidence of a fairly pervasive phenomenon in the business community now becomes quite tempting. Certainly the three groups in question cover a broad range of employment and environmental circumstances. They would not ordinarily be expected to produce the kind of similarity in earnings experiences observed unless some fundamental market or institutional forces were more generally at work in the economy. Despite substantial differences in the *level* of top executive rewards among firms of varying sizes and orientations, then, the pace of *increases* in those rewards has been notably consistent across sectors and over time.

The relationship of the current figures to the large-manufacturing findings deserves particular scrutiny. It happens that the more vigorous rate of appreciation of salary and bonus payments in the smaller companies has been accompanied by a relatively less intensive degree of income supplementation through deferred and contingent compensation arrangements. The effect, as we have seen, is to produce neatly a total pay package displaying virtually the same proportionate net increase since 1940. This outcome is portrayed in Table 11 and Chart 9, and may be summarized as follows:

SALARY PLUS BONUS AS A PER CENT OF TOTAL
AFTER-TAX COMPENSATION

	Large Manufacturers		Small Manufacturers	
	1940–49	1955–63	1940–49	1956–63
Top Executives	72%	38%	87%	60%
Top Five Executives	80	52	91	72

The influence of a lighter burden of progressive personal income taxes on the more modest absolute direct cash rewards of the small-manufacturing sample obviously underlies these figures. A corresponding

TABLE 11

Elements of After-Tax Compensation:
Small Manufacturing Sample, 1940–63
(amounts in dollars)

	Top Executive		Top Five Executives	
Year	Salary and Bonus	Noncurrent Rewards	Salary and Bonus	Noncurrent Rewards
1940	37,264 (99)	418 (1)	24,207 (99)	295 (1)
1941	31,744 (96)	1,457 (4)	21,555 (98)	533 (2)
1942	27,996 (95)	1,485 (5)	19,693 (97)	534 (3)
1943	24,329 (91)	2,262 (9)	17,431 (97)	600 (3)
1944	24,492 (87)	3,509 (13)	17,592 (93)	1,399 (7)
1945	24,444 (91)	2,426 (9)	17,933 (91)	1,684 (9)
1946	28,342 (92)	2,535 (8)	21,196 (93)	1,690 (7)
1947	29,787 (77)	8,829 (23)	22,662 (83)	4,500 (17)
1948	41,114 (88)	5,481 (12)	29,073 (89)	3,534 (11)
1949	38,530 (68)	18,385 (32)	28,656 (83)	5,951 (17)
1950	42,722 (82)	9,150 (18)	29,256 (87)	4,472 (13)
1951	41,668 (84)	7,693 (16)	30,541 (88)	4,047 (12)
1952	40,994 (83)	8,366 (17)	30,012 (88)	4,094 (12)
1953	39,634 (66)	20,717 (34)	29,582 (77)	8,742 (23)
1954	41,881 (64)	23,591 (36)	31,082 (77)	9,142 (23)
1955	42,594 (66)	21,650 (34)	32,164 (77)	9,690 (23)
1956	46,128 (54)	38,998 (46)	33,726 (68)	16,009 (32)
1957	43,652 (56)	33,996 (44)	33,861 (73)	12,401 (27)
1958	44,088 (63)	25,425 (37)	33,761 (76)	10,696 (24)
1959	46,444 (69)	20,445 (31)	35,653 (74)	12,263 (26)
1960	45,638 (65)	24,527 (35)	36,260 (71)	14,992 (29)
1961	44,475 (67)	21,947 (33)	35,722 (73)	13,371 (27)
1962	43,077 (46)	51,409 (54)	37,604 (65)	19,855 (35)
1963	46,858 (71)	18,692 (29)	38,423 (79)	9,991 (21)
Average:				
1940–49	30,804 (87)	4,679 (13)	22,000 (91)	2,072 (9)
1956–63	45,045 (60)	29,430 (40)	35,626 (72)	13,698 (28)

NOTE: Numbers in parentheses denote per cent of total each year.

CHART 9

ELEMENTS OF TOTAL AFTER-TAX COMPENSATION: SMALL MANUFACTURING SAMPLE, 1940-63

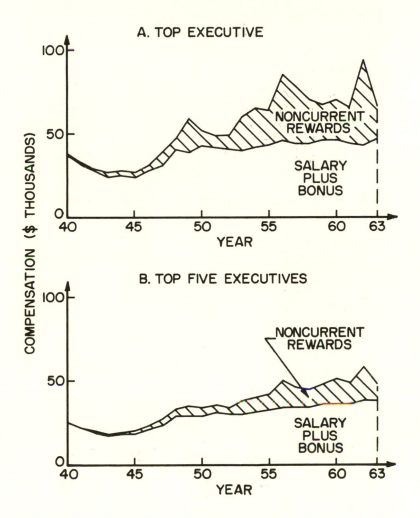

point can be made in connection with the composition of retail trade executives' earnings, which in the aggregate were somewhat under the comparable large industrial levels and were—presumably in response to the tax situation—comprised more heavily of salaries and bonuses. The logic of tax planning in the design of corporate pay policies, therefore, seems to be reflected consistently in the patterns which emerge.[16]

An additional type of consistency is discernible in the hierarchical structure of compensation in the manufacturing sector. The salary-plus-bonus profile among the top five managerial positions turns out to be almost identical for small and large enterprises. Thus, we have:

BEFORE-TAX SALARY PLUS BONUS AS A PER CENT OF
TOP EXECUTIVE'S SALARY PLUS BONUS

Executive Ranks *	Large Manufacturers		Small Manufacturers	
	1940–41	1955–63	1940–41	1956–63
#1	100%	100%	100%	100%
#2	63	75	62	71
#3	50	64	52	61
#4	45	57	45	55
#5	38	53	39	50

* By salary-plus-bonus receipts.

Except for a very minor 2 to 3 percentage point difference in the more recent figures, both the initial and final pay relationships match up extremely well between the two samples. The experience of either one offers a sharp contrast to the much tighter compensation pattern in retail trade organizations.

[16] Further evidence of such planning was uncovered in the original compensation study of large manufacturers, where it turned out that the firms which provided the highest levels of reward for their executives were precisely the firms which utilized deferred and contingent pay schemes most extensively. When companies were ranked within particular periods first by the size of their top executives' earnings and then by the percentage of the latter which was attributable to noncurrent arrangements, correlation coefficients between the rankings on the order of .9 were obtained. See Lewellen, *op. cit.*, pp. 253–254.

Rather less over-all similarity in policies within manufacturing is implied by the aggregate after-tax remuneration data, but the relevant profiles in the two instances have, at least, been maintained intact since prior to World War II:

TOTAL AFTER-TAX COMPENSATION AS A PER CENT OF
TOP EXECUTIVE'S TOTAL AFTER-TAX COMPENSATION

Executive Rank *	Large Manufacturers		Small Manufacturers	
	1940–41	1955–63	1940–41	1956–63
#1	100%	100%	100%	100%
#2	65	67	69	72
#3	53	55	61	60
#4	45	44	52	52
#5	39	38	47	47

* By total compensation.

The widespread uniformity of historical growth rates in total manufacturing executive earnings thereby appears again as an important characteristic of the compensation process.

Because of that uniformity, the senior officers of small firms can be observed to have experienced the same sort of decline in income over the years relative to other professional groups and to hourly production workers that the large-firm findings suggested. In like manner, the corporations involved in the current sample grew noticeably more rapidly since 1940 than did their executives' annual remuneration, though the differences here are not quite as pronounced as is the case in the larger industrials. The record is:

COMPOUND ANNUAL RATES OF GROWTH, 1940–63

A. The 15 Sample Companies (aggregate data):

Assets	5.1%
Sales	7.7
Profits, Before Taxes	5.8
Profits, After Taxes	4.3
Equity Market Value	5.4

B. After-Tax Earnings, Other Groups:

Physicians	5.2%
Lawyers	3.9
Dentists	5.2
Production Workers	5.5

C. Total After-Tax Compensation, Small-Firm Executives: [17]

Top Executives	3.0%
Top Five Executives	3.0

Indeed, at a 3.4 per cent compound annual rate of growth, the Consumer Price Index has outpaced the gains in the indicated managerial earnings during the interval considered, leaving real income for the sample *below* counterpart 1940 levels.

The significant historical difference between the figures for the small and large industrial companies, however, lies in the extent to which stock-based compensation devices have been relied upon as instruments of executive reward. Table 12 and Chart 10 illustrate the point, the dimensions of which are apparent from the following summary:

STOCK-BASED REWARDS AS A PER CENT OF
TOTAL AFTER-TAX COMPENSATION

Executive Rank *	Large Manufacturers 1955–63	Small Manufacturers 1956–63
#1	44%	11%
#2	34	10
#3	31	7
#4	23	5
#5	19	6

* By total compensation.

Interestingly, all the stock-based earnings shown for the smaller companies were accounted for by stock options. None of the fifteen firms studied had either a profit-sharing or a deferred compensation plan utilizing employer-corporation common shares as the means of

[17] The 1956–63 averages shown in Table 10 are used as the 1963 terminal values in these computations.

TABLE 12

Components of Total After-Tax Compensation:
Small Manufacturing Sample, 1940–63
(amounts in dollars)

	Top Executive		Top Five Executives	
Year	Earnings from Fixed-Dollar Rewards	Earnings from Stock-Based Rewards	Earnings from Fixed-Dollar Rewards	Earnings from Stock-Based Rewards
1940	37,682 (100)	— (0)	24,502 (100)	— (0)
1941	32,168 (97)	1,033 (3)	21,854 (99)	235 (1)
1942	28,746 (98)	735 (2)	20,055 (99)	172 (1)
1943	26,030 (98)	561 (2)	17,896 (99)	134 (1)
1944	28,001 (100)	— (0)	18,991 (100)	— (0)
1945	26,870 (100)	— (0)	19,617 (100)	— (0)
1946	30,877 (100)	— (0)	22,886 (100)	— (0)
1947	38,616 (100)	— (0)	27,162 (100)	— (0)
1948	46,595 (100)	— (0)	32,607 (100)	— (0)
1949	56,915 (100)	— (0)	34,607 (100)	— (0)
1950	51,872 (100)	— (0)	33,728 (100)	— (0)
1951	49,361 (100)	— (0)	34,588 (100)	— (0)
1952	49,323 (100)	37 (0)	34,041 (100)	65 (0)
1953	59,910 (99)	441 (1)	38,057 (99)	267 (1)
1954	65,309 (100)	163 (0)	40,174 (100)	50 (0)
1955	60,972 (95)	3,272 (5)	40,310 (96)	1,544 (4)
1956	81,355 (96)	3,771 (4)	47,647 (96)	2,087 (4)
1957	70,581 (91)	7,067 (9)	44,235 (96)	2,026 (4)
1958	64,311 (93)	5,202 (7)	43,048 (97)	1,409 (3)
1959	59,800 (89)	7,089 (11)	43,329 (90)	4,588 (10)
1960	59,258 (84)	10,907 (16)	44,734 (87)	6,517 (13)
1961	59,905 (90)	6,517 (10)	44,133 (90)	4,959 (10)
1962	74,496 (79)	19,990 (21)	49,094 (85)	8,364 (15)
1963	62,017 (95)	3,533 (5)	45,938 (95)	2,476 (5)
Average: 1956–63	66,465 (89)	8,010 (11)	45,271 (92)	4,053 (8)

NOTE: Numbers in parentheses denote per cent of total each year.

CHART 10

COMPONENTS OF TOTAL AFTER-TAX COMPENSATION: SMALL MANUFACTURING SAMPLE, 1940-63

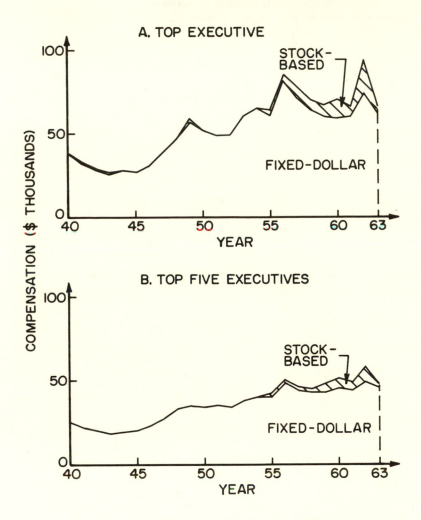

payment. Moreover, because options themselves were substantially less of a factor than was true for large manufacturing executives, only a minor portion of total pay for the current group can be categorized as ownership-related. This observation will be seen to fit into a broader set of relationships between the samples, whose features will become apparent upon examination of executives' stockholdings.

Summary

The foregoing findings trace out a system of historical compensation patterns which indicates a considerable degree of similarity in earnings growth rates among diverse aggregations of senior corporate officials. The key elements of that experience are salary-plus-bonus payments on the one hand, and total annual after-tax remuneration on the other. Indices of the latter were generated by applying the "current income equivalent" concept discussed in the preceding chapter to the compensation information contained in company proxy statements. The results, which involve a wide range of enterprises, suggest a level of consistency in pay policies across firms that should permit some confidence in interpreting many of them as general attributes of the business community.

In particular, we discover a remarkable resemblance between the large and small industrial samples, both in terms of the pace of secular increases in income, and in the intra-firm hierarchical structure of rewards. The retail trade evidence displays a somewhat different set of internal characteristics, but nonetheless traces out over-all historical rates of growth which match quite closely the corresponding manufacturing figures.[18] The proportionate representation in the total pay package of fixed-dollar and stock-based sources of earnings was identified as a starting point for our analysis of the shareholder-management income link. Having laid that foundation, and having provided a body of compensation data against which to measure the importance of other income items, we may now proceed to consider the consequences of the executive stock ownership phenomenon.

[18] While the investigation thus far has dealt only with the mean values of the various receipts at issue, the dispersion about those means will also be treated in the discussions which follow.

4

STOCK OWNERSHIP AND INCOME: LARGE MANUFACTURERS

SEVERAL DIMENSIONS of senior corporate executives' holdings of their employer firms' common shares are of concern in appraising the management-shareholder relationship. The magnitude of the relevant equity investments, the pattern of increases in those investments over the years, and the associated dividend and capital appreciation returns, are among the most significant features of the historical record. The experience of the top management group in the fifty firms which constitute what has been designated here the "large manufacturing" sample will be the initial focus for an examination of that record.

Stockholdings

The men in the indicated sample turn out to have been shareholders of substantial proportions in their own companies. Table 13 lists the means of the market values of the pertinent holdings as of the start of every year from 1940 to 1963. The figures were obtained by multiplying January 1 stockholdings by the corresponding January 1 market prices,[1] and data are presented for the average of both the highest-paid, and the five highest-paid, executive positions in each firm. Chart 11 depicts the findings.

We observe that during the early 1940's, the typical portfolio commitment to the common shares of one's own company ran in the neighborhood of $400,000 to $600,000 per capita for the group examined. While, even at that level, these were clearly not inconsequential investments, the same averages had reached as much

---

[1] Actually, the immediately preceding December 31 closing prices were used, as was noted in the methodological discussion in Chapter 2.

TABLE 13

Average Market Value of Executive Stockholdings: Large Manufacturing Sample, 1940–63
(amounts in dollars)

Year	Top Executive	Top Five Executives
1940	682,502	574,743
1941	544,599	482,267
1942	315,819	363,013
1943	333,339	392,891
1944	385,107	427,821
1945	776,553	492,254
1946	708,668	389,629
1947	511,150	238,310
1948	486,597	231,318
1949	421,314	201,886
1950	469,428	232,994
1951	720,040	321,783
1952	640,840	344,438
1953	687,144	383,363
1954	634,474	341,437
1955	1,131,830	522,320
1956	1,346,068	733,359
1957	989,553	962,243
1958	1,077,381	973,250
1959	1,523,092	1,461,881
1960	1,685,288	1,932,440
1961	2,050,280	1,879,604
1962	3,256,440	3,033,896
1963	2,624,557	2,365,847

NOTE: Figures are as of January 1 of each year.

CHART II

MARKET VALUE OF EXECUTIVE STOCKHOLDINGS:
LARGE MANUFACTURING SAMPLE, 1940-63

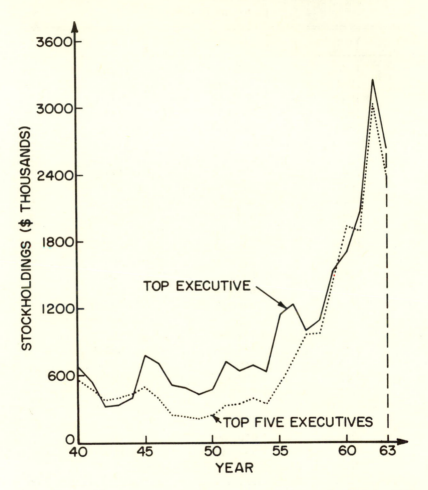

as $2 million to $3 million per executive by the early 1960's. This kind of exposure to the contingencies of ownership would be difficult to reject out of hand as unlikely to have some influence on the managerial decision process; it should engender some sympathy and concern for the welfare of shareholders. There appears to be no striking difference in the figures for the top and top-five categories shown, suggesting that the chief executive in a firm is by no means the only individual whose income permits him to indulge a taste for what amounts to investing in his own abilities.[2] Similarly, the volatility of the two sets of annual averages, especially in the later years tabulated, implies that both officer categories have been subject to strong and direct securities market effects on personal net worth.

Dividend Income

The dividend receipts occasioned by the recorded ownership patterns have played an important role in the executive income structure. Table 14 indicates that mean annual pre-tax dividends for the sample were in the $30,000 range prior to World War II; that they declined to approximately half that figure during the war; but that by 1963, they had risen steadily to a rate of slightly over $70,000 per man. Again, the disparities between the top and top-five findings are minor.

The relationship between these receipts and the before-tax salary-plus-bonus earnings of the same individuals is portrayed in Table 15. At the levels in question, dividends averaged roughly one-third of direct cash compensation in the early 1960's for the highest-paid executive in each company, up from 20 per cent or less in the early 1940's. The counterpart gain for the five highest-paid combined was from an initial one-third to just under one-half by the end of the interval studied. The point was made earlier that in estimating effective tax rates on managerial pay in the compensation calculations, income from sources other than employment was set equal to 15 per cent of the man's salary-plus-bonus payments for the year.[3] The numbers in Table 15 obviously imply that such an estimate is too conservative, unless it can be argued that fairly sizeable interest deductions from taxable income arise from personal loans undertaken to support investments of the magnitude at issue. That argument *will* be accepted here, for the reasons discussed in Chapter 2, but a

---

[2] Were the men ranked within companies by the size of their stockholdings instead of their total after-tax compensation, a sharper gradient in the ownership averages by position would, of course, emerge.

[3] See pp. 27–30.

TABLE 14

Average Dividend Receipts:
Large Manufacturing Sample, 1940–63
(amounts in dollars)

Year	Top Executive		Top Five Executives	
	Before Taxes	After Taxes	Before Taxes	After Taxes
1940	29,976	17,749	30,815	17,639
1941	28,253	13,808	30,331	14,368
1942	16,658	6,101	20,490	7,820
1943	16,135	4,976	18,379	5,836
1944	17,911	5,511	21,742	6,781
1945	34,287	10,263	21,579	6,685
1946	23,669	9,280	13,343	5,326
1947	27,150	10,297	12,580	5,178
1948	30,589	15,870	14,035	7,656
1949	31,730	16,026	14,533	7,678
1950	37,602	18,880	18,598	9,567
1951	43,068	20,385	18,848	9,514
1952	31,675	13,913	18,151	8,506
1953	32,689	14,512	18,839	8,886
1954	38,665	18,080	20,644	10,012
1955	50,559	22,918	23,090	11,051
1956	50,799	23,234	27,728	13,294
1957	33,803	15,079	30,436	14,416
1958	40,919	18,100	33,823	16,417
1959	41,662	18,404	36,044	17,506
1960	43,292	19,287	41,210	20,602
1961	44,756	19,810	45,595	22,238
1962	56,780	23,825	65,924	30,640
1963	73,466	31,212	71,363	32,755

TABLE 15

Mean Before-Tax Dividend Receipts as a Per Cent of Mean Before-Tax Salary Plus Bonus: Large Manufacturing Sample, 1940–63

Year	Top Executive	Top Five Executives
1940	22	38
1941	20	36
1942	12	24
1943	11	21
1944	13	25
1945	26	25
1946	18	15
1947	19	13
1948	20	14
1949	19	13
1950	22	16
1951	26	16
1952	18	14
1953	19	14
1954	22	15
1955	28	16
1956	27	18
1957	18	20
1958	22	24
1959	22	25
1960	23	29
1961	24	33
1962	31	46
1963	37	48

sensitivity analysis of the possible consequences of its being inappropriate will be presented below.

Those consequences relate primarily to the after-tax dividend record, which is also presented in Table 14. If executives' total currently taxable income has been understated, both the listed figures and the after-tax salary-plus-bonus receipts calculated previously will err on the high side, i.e., the attendant personal tax liabilities will have been determined in conjunction with too low a set of progressive individual marginal rate brackets. Assuming for the moment that no substantial errors have, in fact, been introduced, we find that post-tax dividend inflows grew from about $15,000 annually for senior executives in 1940 and 1941 to $30,000 or more by 1963.

Capital Gains

The complementary item of ownership income consists of the annual capital gains generated by the stockholdings involved. In conformity with the viewpoint expressed in Chapter 2, accrued as well as realized gains—and losses—are taken to be relevant to an appraisal of the secular impact of those holdings on personal net worth. Accordingly, the annual pre-tax increments to executives' wealth occasioned by their equity investments in their companies' common shares are shown in Table 16, together with the after-tax increments which are implied by the effective capital gains tax rate of 15 per cent that was decided upon earlier as an appropriate estimate.[4] Chart 12 depicts the after-tax figures.

Unquestionably, the annual magnitudes are impressive, particularly in the more recent years tabulated. Post-tax gains and losses were generally in the $40,000 to $60,000 per capita range during the early 1940's, but from the mid-1950's on, have expanded to anywhere from $100,000 to $750,000 each year for the typical executive. The feeling here is that changes in wealth on that scale should at least begin to sensitize even the most callous professional manager to the

[4] This estimate, it will be recalled, is less than 25 per cent as a reflection of the deferral of tax liabilities on accrued gains and the possibility of tax avoidance through retention of the stock until death. See pp. 25–27, and Bailey, op. cit.

TABLE 16

Average Capital Gains:
Large Manufacturing Sample, 1940–63
(amounts in dollars)

Year	Top Executive		Top Five Executives	
	Before Taxes	After Taxes	Before Taxes	After Taxes
1940	−72,006	−61,205	−74,851	−63,623
1941	−61,455	−52,236	−102,100	−86,785
1942	41,617	35,374	73,838	62,762
1943	54,872	46,641	59,689	50,735
1944	72,792	61,873	75,313	64,016
1945	212,559	180,675	119,889	101,905
1946	−84,011	−71,409	−47,537	−40,406
1947	8,476	7,204	5,312	4,515
1948	7,139	6,068	−3,417	−2,904
1949	98,613	83,821	42,310	35,963
1950	148,628	126,333	67,403	57,292
1951	159,230	135,345	54,581	46,393
1952	57,569	48,933	40,839	34,713
1953	−58,305	−49,559	−23,930	−20,340
1954	368,532	313,252	209,798	178,328
1955	267,233	227,148	124,859	106,130
1956	158,906	135,070	97,976	83,279
1957	−149,881	−127,398	−98,778	−83,961
1958	458,493	389,719	451,948	384,155
1959	193,374	164,367	263,113	223,646
1960	−119,204	−101,323	−122,066	−103,756
1961	786,968	668,922	547,128	465,058
1962	−885,513	−752,686	−630,360	−535,806
1963	725,238	616,452	549,239	466,853

CHART 12

AVERAGE ANNUAL AFTER-TAX CAPITAL GAINS:
LARGE MANUFACTURING SAMPLE, 1940-63

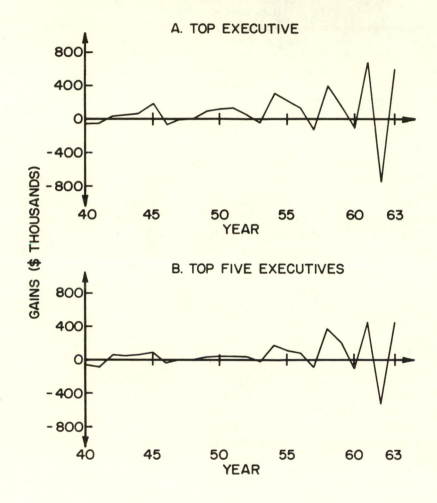

shareholder viewpoint. The price fluctuations which have occurred in the securities markets since 1963 suggest that comparable annual figures would emerge if the data were extended to the present.[5]

While these findings, as they stand, identify a rather strong owner-ship-management income relationship, a still more accurate appreciation of that phenomenon can be provided. There is the possibility that in aggregating the various increments to personal net worth across the sample within a given year, declines in the market value of certain executives' stockholdings may offset concurrent increases experienced by their counterparts in other firms. A $100,000 capital loss by one man, for example, may cancel, in the totals, a $100,000 gain by another and lead to an under-reporting of the actual per capita change in wealth for the group.[6] On that chance, the *absolute* values of the respective annual increments were averaged and the results are displayed in Table 17. We observe that the majority of the figures are raised by this procedure, but not to any substantial degree. Apparently, the stock prices of the fifty corporations examined moved fairly consistently in the same direction throughout the interval under scrutiny. Because the absolute figures seem to address the issue of over-all impact on executives somewhat more precisely and more conveniently than do the net figures contained in Table 16, the former will be utilized hereafter in most instances when establishing comparisons with executives' compensation.

Compensation and Ownership Income

Perhaps the most illuminating such comparison is that offered by Tables 18 and 19, where the major components of executive income are brought together. On the one hand are tabulated the mean annual

---

[5] It may be noted that the before-tax capital gains listed do not simply represent the successive differences in the January 1 shareholdings from Table 13. They represent instead the capital gains enjoyed—or losses suffered—during the year under consideration by the individuals who, at the *beginning* of that year, occupied the five highest-paid positions in the sample companies. Since the following January 1 frequently finds a new set of men in those positions, their holdings will not ordinarily have the same market value on that date as the holdings of the group which immediately preceded them.

[6] This problem was discussed earlier, in Chapter 2.

TABLE 17

Average Absolute Capital Gains:
Large Manufacturing Sample, 1940–63
(amounts in dollars)

Year	Top Executive		Top Five Executives	
	Before Taxes	After Taxes	Before Taxes	After Taxes
1940	75,291	63,997	77,917	66,229
1941	65,152	55,379	104,467	88,796
1942	69,849	59,371	95,118	80,850
1943	99,511	84,584	82,691	70,287
1944	74,061	62,951	76,952	65,409
1945	212,559	180,675	119,889	101,905
1946	100,057	85,048	63,702	54,146
1947	95,481	81,158	34,113	28,996
1948	39,586	33,648	18,173	15,447
1949	113,136	96,165	48,447	41,179
1950	160,524	136,445	74,243	63,106
1951	181,903	154,617	66,374	56,417
1952	92,765	78,850	54,936	46,695
1953	99,107	84,240	46,732	39,722
1954	368,532	313,252	209,798	178,328
1955	284,683	241,980	132,545	112,663
1956	244,543	207,861	148,443	126,176
1957	183,564	156,029	178,707	151,900
1958	459,454	390,535	456,111	387,694
1959	261,945	222,653	351,440	298,724
1960	400,462	340,392	466,927	396,887
1961	811,500	689,775	747,756	635,592
1962	926,982	787,934	786,985	668,937
1963	739,938	628,947	559,936	475,945

TABLE 18

Compensation and Ownership Income:
Large Manufacturing Sample, 1940–63;
Average for the Top Executive in Each Firm

Year	Compensation		Ownership Income		Comparison	
	(1) After-Tax Fixed-Dollar Remuneration	(2) After-Tax Stock-Based Remuneration	(3) After-Tax Dividend Income	(4) Absolute After-Tax Capital Gains	(5) $\frac{[(3)+(4)]}{[(1)+(2)]}$	(6) $\frac{[(2)+(3)+(4)]}{(1)}$
1940	$ 98,755	$ 3,224	$17,749	$ 63,997	0.802	0.860
1941	88,776	2,759	13,809	55,379	0.756	0.810
1942	63,864	2,096	6,101	59,371	0.993	1.058
1943	54,467	1,994	4,976	84,584	1.586	1.681
1944	62,353	1,314	5,511	62,951	1.075	1.119
1945	60,682	950	10,263	180,675	3.098	3.162
1946	68,295	748	9,280	85,048	1.366	1.392
1947	77,693	624	10,297	81,158	1.168	1.185
1948	97,379	2,375	15,870	33,648	0.496	0.533
1949	99,450	5,861	16,026	96,165	1.065	1.187
1950	113,944	8,846	18,880	136,445	1.265	1.441
1951	99,317	10,024	20,385	154,617	1.601	1.863
1952	96,563	20,094	13,913	78,850	0.795	1.169
1953	102,072	29,710	14,512	84,240	0.749	1.259
1954	110,582	32,888	18,080	313,252	2.309	3.294
1955	130,450	83,980	22,918	241,980	1.235	2.674
1956	125,208	110,466	23,234	207,861	0.980	2.728
1957	127,552	99,675	15,079	156,029	0.753	2.123
1958	115,935	52,872	18,100	390,535	2.420	3.981
1959	121,837	92,173	18,404	222,653	1.126	2.735
1960	116,445	108,408	19,287	340,392	1.600	4.020
1961	111,100	96,019	19,810	689,775	3.426	7.251
1962	115,906	112,326	23,825	787,934	3.557	7.973
1963	107,596	82,228	31,212	628,947	3.478	6.900
Averages:						
1940–44	$ 73,643	$ 2,277	$ 9,629	$ 65,256	0.986	1.048
1960–63	112,762	99,745	23,534	611,762	2.990	6.519

TABLE 19

Compensation and Ownership Income:
Large Manufacturing Sample, 1940–63;
Average for the Top Five Executives in Each Firm

	Compensation		Ownership Income		Comparison	
	(1) After- Tax Fixed- Dollar Remu- Year	(2) After- Tax Stock- Based Remu- neration	(3) After- Tax Dividend Income	(4) Absolute After- Tax Capital Gains	(5) $\frac{[(3)+(4)]}{[(1)+(2)]}$	(6) $\frac{[(2)+(3)+(4)]}{(1)}$
1940	$56,904	$ 2,769	$17,639	$ 66,229	1.405	1.523
1941	54,757	2,262	14,368	88,796	1.809	1.925
1942	42,787	1,759	7,820	80,850	1.991	2.113
1943	37,486	1,534	5,836	70,287	1.951	2.072
1944	40,787	933	6,781	65,409	1.730	1.793
1945	40,780	667	6,685	101,905	2.620	2.679
1946	46,974	945	5,326	54,146	1.241	1.286
1947	49,306	601	5,178	28,996	0.685	0.705
1948	66,028	1,400	7,656	15,447	0.343	0.371
1949	68,202	2,575	7,678	41,179	0.690	0.754
1950	75,146	3,849	9,567	63,106	0.920	1.018
1951	72,843	4,524	9,514	56,417	0.852	0.967
1952	70,791	8,760	8,506	46,695	0.694	0.904
1953	74,242	11,740	8,886	39,722	0.565	0.813
1954	80,811	12,456	10,012	178,328	2.019	2.485
1955	90,332	34,679	11,051	112,663	0.990	1.753
1956	89,153	47,212	13,294	126,176	1.023	2.094
1957	90,023	42,820	14,416	151,900	1.252	2.323
1958	84,322	24,623	16,417	387,694	3.709	5.084
1959	85,779	45,383	17,506	298,724	2.411	4.216
1960	83,727	49,737	20,602	396,887	3.128	5.580
1961	81,657	50,015	22,238	635,592	4.996	8.669
1962	85,854	53,390	30,640	668,937	5.024	8.770
1963	84,357	37,191	32,755	475,945	4.185	6.471
Averages:						
1940–44	$46,544	$ 1,851	$10,489	$ 74,314	1.752	1.862
1960–63	83,899	47,583	26,559	544,340	4.342	7.372

after-tax earnings experienced in the form of employee remuneration by the men in the sample. They are comprised of the fixed-dollar and stock-based rewards treated in Chapter 3, the sum of which defines total after-tax compensation each year at each position. On the other side are the two elements of the same individuals' direct ownership benefits—the mean after-tax dividend receipts and the absolute after-tax capital gains just recorded. The relationships between these four sources of increments to personal net worth permit a comprehensive assessment of the role which ownership-related items play in the combined structure of managerial income.

The figures very clearly document the preeminence of stock-associated returns. Annual ownership income flows roughly matched total annual compensation for the highest-paid executives in the fifty firms in the early years studied (column 5 of Table 18). By the 1960's, however, the balance had shifted to approximately three-to-one in favor of dividends and capital gains. For the five highest-paid men as a group (column 5 of Table 19), the proportions are approximately two-to-one and four-to-one, respectively.[7] In addition to the fact that in almost *every* year the level of executives' participation in ownership returns is substantial, the historical trend runs counter to the usual view that a steady process of disengagement has occurred as a result of the professionalization of management. It will be recalled, of course, that the category of firms in question—large organizations with a wide public stock distribution and no dominant shareholder bloc—is precisely that which is most often cited as an extreme example of allegedly deleterious ownership-management separation.

The comparisons indicated, however, still understate the case. Because a portion of senior executives' earnings is itself attributable to stock-based arrangements, the appropriate focus for our purposes here should be the relationships tabulated in column 6 of the two tables. While little different from their counterparts in column 5 in

[7] The relatively greater importance of ownership elements for the top-five officer contingent follows from the evidence that the stockholding gradient in the managerial hierarchy is less pronounced than is the compensation gradient. See Tables 2 and 13.

the 1940's, these figures show that the changes in managerial net worth generated by the combination of annual dividends, capital gains, and stock-related pay schemes outweighed the only real non-ownership income source—fixed-dollar rewards—by ratios of anywhere from six-to-one to eight-to-one during the early 1960's. We, therefore, are dealing with a group of individuals who are frequently confronted with annual per capita employer-company increments to personal wealth in the $700,000 range after taxes, more than $600,000 of which can be traced in some fashion to dividend payments and market share price changes. On its surface, this does not seem the kind of circumstance which would lead one to believe that executives are apt to become indifferent to the legitimate interests of shareholders. Indeed, over time, the apparent tendency is toward a growing harmony of pecuniary objectives.

Sensitivity of the Results

The issue was raised earlier that certain of the assumptions made, and parameters chosen, in performing the computations on which the foregoing comparisons are based might reasonably be open to argument. The stipulation that 15 per cent rather than 25 per cent was a fair approximation of the effective capital gains tax rate for executives, and that their current taxable income from sources other than employment amounted to 15 per cent of direct cash salary and bonus receipts, were the two major points of concern. The second of these was, as we have seen, cast into particular doubt by the evidence of sizeable dividend income on the part of senior management. The question which must be addressed, then, is whether a different decision about either parameter would significantly alter the tone or strength of the findings just presented.

In that regard, we may inquire initially as to the impact of specifying instead the full statutory capital gains rate of 25 per cent, which would cause a uniform reduction in the after-tax figures representing the dominant portion of executives' "ownership income" flows. The following summary indicates the consequences for both the very earliest and the very latest years covered by the study:

OWNERSHIP INCOME AND COMPENSATION, 1940–44 AND 1960–63

	Annual Averages			
	Top Executive		Top Five Executives	
Item	1940–44	1960–63	1940–44	1960–63
After-Tax Dividends Plus Absolute After-Tax Capital Gains:				
a. 15% Gains Tax Rate	$74,885	$635,296	$84,803	$570,899
b. 25% Gains Tax Rate	57,578	539,790	65,571	480,300
Ratio of Dividends Plus Absolute Gains to Total After-Tax Executive Compensation:				
a. 15% Gains Tax Rate	0.986	2.990	1.752	4.342
b. 25% Gains Tax Rate	0.885	2.651	1.572	3.855
Ratio of Dividends Plus Absolute Gains Plus Stock-Related Compensation to Fixed-Dollar Compensation				
a. 15% Gains Tax Rate	1.048	6.519	1.862	7.372
b. 25% Gains Tax Rate	0.944	5.880	1.674	6.608

While the relative importance of ownership income necessarily diminishes under the revised tax assumption, the change is quite modest and the orders of magnitude of the key ratios are still more than adequate to support the basic contention of the analysis. Since 25 per cent is, of course, the maximum possible capital gains rate, the comparison offered here is the *least* favorable one that could be generated.

Equally reassuring results emerge from considering the potential effect of having underestimated executives' total currently taxable income. As has been discussed, too low a prediction of that figure would lead to imputations of too light a tax burden on salary and bonus payments as well as on the dividend receipts executives enjoy, causing, perhaps, a distortion in the relationships between the several items. A convenient way to test that possibility is simply to reduce both income components by a given percentage, and to examine the changes thereby produced in the comparative weights of top management's ownership returns and compensation. If we concentrate again on the key early-1940's and early-1960's periods, lowering in each instance after-tax salary plus bonus earnings (from Table 3) and after-tax dividends (Table 14), first by 10 per cent and then by 20 per cent across the board, the outcome is as portrayed in Table 20.

Whereas an increase in the assumed effective capital gains tax rate operated to dilute slightly the conclusions drawn on the preceding pages, the recognition of possible higher ordinary tax liabilities turns out to *reinforce* those conclusions very consistently. The original ratios of ownership-connected income elements to nonownership earnings are raised in every instance by the revisions. The explanation lies simply in the fact that salaries and bonuses comprise a larger share of both total and fixed-dollar managerial compensation than do dividends of aggregate ownership returns. Any change in parameters which creates a heavier tax burden on ordinary income receipts will therefore end up augmenting the relative weight of ownership items vis-à-vis employee compensation.

The approach taken here in attempting to assess the possible extent of such changes is merely a proxy for the fuller procedure of actually changing the "outside income" estimate of 15 per cent, redoing the various tax calculations, and coming up with a new set of comparisons on the basis of the modified figures. Since the effect of that procedure would necessarily be to reduce after-tax salaries, bonuses, and dividends in matching proportions, the simpler test implemented in Table 20 serves our purposes as well. Certainly, a 20 per cent drop in the after-tax figures would require a substantial increase in assumed taxable income in order to generate the higher tax levies which are implied. The consequent changes in the several ownership-compensation ratios may, accordingly, be interpreted as the extremes of the range of potential revisions. In any event, it is clear that if errors have been made in specifying too low an effective capital gains tax rate, and too low a taxable income estimate, those errors are offsetting and will, in combination, have a very minor impact on the compari-

TABLE 20

Impact of Changes in Tax Estimates: Large Manufacturing Sample,
1940–44 and 1960–63

	Annual Averages			
	Top Executive		Top Five Executives	
Item	1940–44	1960–63	1940–44	1960–63
After-Tax Salary Plus Bonus:				
a. Original Values	$55,226	$ 81,145	$38,856	$ 66,904
b. Less 10%	49,703	73,031	34,970	60,214
c. Less 20%	44,181	64,916	31,085	53,523
After-Tax Dividend Income:				
a. Original Values	9,629	23,534	10,489	26,559
b. Less 10%	8,666	21,181	9,440	23,903
c. Less 20%	7,703	18,827	8,391	21,247
Total After-Tax Compensation:				
a. Original Values	75,920	212,507	48,396	131,483
b. With Salary Down 10%	70,397	204,393	44,510	124,793
c. With Salary Down 20%	64,875	196,278	40,625	118,102
Total Ownership Income: [a]				
a. Original Values	74,885	635,296	84,803	570,899
b. With Dividends Down 10%	73,922	632,943	83,754	568,243
c. With Dividends Down 20%	72,959	630,589	82,705	565,587
Ratio of Ownership Income to Total Compensation:				
a. Original Values	0.986	2.990	1.752	4.342
b. With 10% Adjustments	1.050	3.097	1.882	4.553
c. With 20% Adjustments	1.125	3.213	2.036	4.789
Ratio of Ownership Income Plus Stock-Related Compensation to Fixed-Dollar Compensation:				
a. Original Values	1.048	6.519	1.862	7.372
b. With 10% Adjustments	1.119	7.001	2.007	7.976
c. With 20% Adjustments	1.202	7.566	2.181	8.695

[a] Using absolute capital gains figures.

sons at issue. For that reason, the original evidence seems an appropriate basis for the analysis.

Dispersion of the Data

A rather different sort of sensitivity test does, however, suggest the need for caution in relying entirely on the figures as they stand. Thus far, we have been dealing exclusively with mean values for the sample as measures of a "typical" executive's experience. In that light, if it should turn out that in particular years a small number of individuals within the group studied have owned extraordinarily large amounts of their firms' stock, those holdings might well influence the averages disproportionately. Because the sample does include various firms—DuPont, IBM, Firestone Tire, General Tire, and several others—with some degree of family owner-manager tradition, and the often attendant element of inherited wealth, the chance of a few scattered large equity portfolios distorting the findings cannot be ignored.

To guard against overstating the argument, it appears desirable, therefore, to identify and segregate any such extreme observations. For that purpose, the standard deviations of the distributions across the fifty corporations of the stockholding market values within each of the five executive positions were computed for each of the twenty-four years examined. All individuals whose holdings in a given year exceeded by two standard deviations or more the original means for their positions were then removed from the sample in that year and a new mean calculated from the remaining figures. A two-standard-deviation hurdle was chosen quite arbitrarily, reflecting its wide use in statistical testing as a criterion for specifying extreme cases. The effect, as it happened, was to eliminate from consideration an average of just over two executives at each level in the hierarchy in every year, giving rise to a reduction of roughly 5 per cent in the initial population throughout.[8] Because, in all instances, the outcome of

[8] The revised sample contains 4,996 man-year observations, down from an initial 5,241. As indicated previously, a complete sample would consist of 6,000 man-years (see Chapter 2).

subtracting two standard deviations from the original mean was a negative number, deletions from the sample occurred only at the upper end of the various annual shareholding distributions.

Ownership and Income: Revised Figures

The influence of those extraordinary values is apparent from Table 21, which lists the revised January 1 stockholding means. When these figures are compared with their counterparts in Table 13, we find that a diminution in the averages of anywhere from one-third to one-half has occurred. It would seem that, in fact, a small number of unusually large ownership positions *have* had a powerful effect. On the other hand, it is also evident that the reduced means are in no sense trivial, documenting as they do investments by senior executives in their own companies which run in excess of $1 million per capita in the later years investigated. Personal portfolio commitments of that magnitude, while unquestionably more modest than the original $2 to $3 million levels, still seem sufficient to support the underlying hypothesis of a strong and direct pecuniary link between owners and managers.

The separate elements of that link, according to the new data, are recorded in Appendix D. The dividend payments involved are down by one-third to one-half from the full-sample figures, averaging, after taxes, approximately $16,000 annually at the top executive position, and $14,000 for the top five together, in the early 1960's. The original values for both categories (Table 14) were generally in the $25,000 annual range during the same period. In addition, there is considerably less volatility in the year-to-year figures than was true before—a result which applies also to the revised stockholding market value time series. Thus, the more sizeable individual equity investments on the initial list were apparently among the more sensitive to external market conditions.

The capital gains and losses tabulated in the Appendix reflect this characteristic. The revised average absolute annual after-tax amounts are in the $30,000 to $60,000 bracket in the early 1940's, and vary

TABLE 21

Average Market Value of Executive Stockholdings:
Large Manufacturing Sample, 1940–63;
Extreme Values Deleted
(amounts in dollars)

Year	Top Executive	Top Five Executives
1940	458,756	269,857
1941	346,365	203,914
1942	184,943	168,376
1943	179,293	155,407
1944	217,188	153,379
1945	495,168	199,317
1946	448,317	209,776
1947	305,723	134,459
1948	251,441	125,165
1949	271,248	116,639
1950	270,111	130,146
1951	468,367	194,719
1952	437,972	213,144
1953	414,473	222,259
1954	412,506	211,562
1955	808,255	365,578
1956	964,652	488,815
1957	744,453	556,992
1958	709,390	531,028
1959	1,044,818	807,896
1960	1,088,689	973,436
1961	1,134,304	795,573
1962	1,164,526	1,024,326
1963	1,152,847	861,286

NOTE: Figures are as of January 1 of each year.

from $150,000 to $300,000 after 1960.[9] The latter figures, in particular, represent a substantial decline from the $500,000 or better yearly changes in wealth identified on our first pass through (Tables 16 and 17). The question, then, is whether the new findings vitiate the contention that ownership-related returns dominate the managerial income structure.

Compensation: Revised Figures

In addressing that question, it is necessary, in the interest of consistency, to perform for other income sources the same operation with regard to extremes that was applied to executives' ownership positions. Specifically, meaningful comparisons of the revised dividend and capital gains time series with employee compensation data require first the identification and deletion of extraordinary values in the annual distributions of compensation across the fifty-firm sample. A plus-or-minus 2σ cutoff standard, when imposed on the total after-tax executive pay population at each position each year, yields a reduction in sample size of approximately 6 per cent: from an original 5,241 down to 4,933 observations. Despite the somewhat larger number of deletions on this scale than was true of the stockholding profile, it happens that the impact of their removal on the subsequent averages is rather milder. Thus, there are a few more relatively unusual values in the remuneration figures, but they turn out to be *individually* less extreme than their ownership counterparts. Once again, however, all the unusual cases occur at the top of the relevant distributions, none at the lower end.

The revised annual remuneration means, and the division of those sums between fixed-dollar and stock-based rewards, are shown in Appendix D. While the total pay figures are perhaps 10 to 15 per cent below the initial averages listed in Table 2 above, they continue to suggest that aggregate executive earnings a little better than doubled during the interval examined. They also retain a fairly pronounced volatility from year to year after the mid-1950's, and document a shift

[9] These are, as before, January 1 to December 31 increments, and the effective capital gains tax rate is assumed to be 15 per cent.

over time of approximately the same dimensions toward owner-
ship-oriented forms of compensation. Were these numbers to be used
in place of the original calculations, therefore, our conclusions about
the historical development of executive pay policies in large manufacturing enterprises would not be noticeably altered.

Compensation and Ownership Income:
Revised Comparisons

On the other hand, the relationships between the modified remuneration averages and the similarly defined ownership income figures do
suggest some departures from the earlier patterns observed. To begin
with, dividends now appear to be markedly smaller in comparison with
executives' salary-plus-bonus receipts than was indicated previously.
Table 22 provides the evidence. We see that pre-tax dividend income
from holdings of employer-company shares ran from 12 to 15 per
cent of aggregate direct cash compensation immediately prior to
World War II, rising to slightly above 20 per cent in the early 1960's.
The original proportions (Table 15) were, in most instances, nearly
twice as great. Notwithstanding these declines,[10] dividends still emerge
as a significant earnings source. The new figures also display rather
more stability than did their predecessors, changing from period to
period in a less abrupt manner.

The full comparison between ownership returns and employee
remuneration according to the revised data is presented in Tables 23
and 24 for the top, and top-five, managerial categories, respectively.
We find after-tax dividends plus absolute after-tax capital gains averaging about three-fourths of annual after-tax pay for both groups in
the first few years shown, but rising to some one and one-fourth to
one and three-fourths times compensation from 1960 on (column 5
of the tables). When stock-based rewards are—as they logically
should be—combined with direct ownership income (column 6),
however, the ratios of those flows to fixed-dollar earnings once more

---

[10] Which, parenthetically, would tend to ameliorate the earlier concern that
estimates of executives' total taxable income from all current sources may
have been too conservative.

TABLE 22

Mean Before-Tax Dividend Receipts as a Per Cent of Mean
Before-Tax Salary Plus Bonus: Large Manufacturing Sample,
1940–63; Extreme Values Deleted

Year	Top Executive	Top Five Executives
1940	14	15
1941	12	13
1942	8	11
1943	8	10
1944	10	9
1945	16	10
1946	13	9
1947	11	7
1948	11	8
1949	12	8
1950	13	10
1951	16	10
1952	13	9
1953	12	9
1954	15	10
1955	22	13
1956	20	13
1957	14	14
1958	16	16
1959	16	17
1960	16	18
1961	21	19
1962	20	22
1963	23	22

TABLE 23

Compensation and Ownership Income:
Large Manufacturing Sample, 1940–63;
Average for the Top Executive in Each Firm,
Extreme Values Deleted

Year	Compensation		Ownership Income		Comparison	
	(1) After- Tax Fixed- Dollar Remu- neration	(2) After- Tax Stock- Based Remu- neration	(3) After- Tax Dividend Income	(4) Absolute After- Tax Capital Gains	(5) $\frac{[(3)+(4)]}{[(1)+(2)]}$	(6) $\frac{[(2)+(3)+(4)]}{(1)}$
1940	$ 81,524	$ 3,435	$11,169	$ 50,930	0.731	0.804
1941	75,202	2,876	8,150	43,888	0.666	0.730
1942	58,898	2,185	4,139	31,422	0.582	0.641
1943	52,106	2,079	3,479	64,912	1.262	1.352
1944	56,226	1,369	4,067	42,549	0.809	0.853
1945	55,414	989	6,557	138,680	2.575	2.639
1946	65,348	530	6,832	60,183	1.017	1.034
1947	66,742	664	5,902	40,840	0.693	0.710
1948	91,762	2,474	8,982	18,660	0.293	0.328
1949	92,778	4,960	9,882	49,453	0.607	0.693
1950	106,414	8,378	11,134	83,382	0.823	0.967
1951	94,955	2,522	12,255	71,881	0.863	0.913
1952	92,647	7,910	9,436	68,312	0.773	0.925
1953	101,396	12,970	9,399	47,816	0.500	0.692
1954	105,101	22,990	12,163	219,579	1.809	2.424
1955	119,424	64,855	17,630	187,706	1.114	2.262
1956	124,397	80,061	17,108	166,231	0.897	2.117
1957	128,601	80,437	12,029	122,769	0.645	1.674
1958	109,804	38,769	13,111	299,595	2.105	3.201
1959	119,954	71,946	13,259	122,346	0.707	1.730
1960	115,639	82,178	13,222	227,185	1.215	2.790
1961	111,520	73,473	17,228	314,755	1.795	3.636
1962	116,356	80,575	15,162	155,047	0.864	2.155
1963	107,672	58,708	19,301	185,759	1.232	2.450
Average: 1940–44	$ 64,791	$ 2,389	$ 6,201	$ 46,740	0.788	0.854
1960–63	112,797	73,734	16,228	220,687	1.270	2.754

TABLE 24

Compensation and Ownership Income
Large Manufacturing Sample, 1940–63;
Average for the Top Five Executives
in Each Firm, Extreme Values Deleted

	Compensation		Ownership Income		Comparison	
	(1) After- Tax Fixed- Dollar Remu-	(2) After- Tax Stock- Based Remu-	(3) After- Tax Dividend	(4) Absolute After- Tax Capital	(5) [(3)+(4)]	(6) [(2)+(3)+(4)]
Year	neration	neration	Income	Gains	[(1)+(2)]	(1)
1940	$51,646	$ 1,561	$ 7,361	$ 30,165	0.705	0.757
1941	47,621	1,900	5,515	25,136	0.619	0.684
1942	40,115	1,210	3,867	28,230	0.777	0.830
1943	36,404	688	2,986	34,138	1.001	1.039
1944	38,264	726	2,828	24,791	0.708	0.741
1945	38,227	612	2,901	52,511	1.427	1.466
1946	43,722	587	3,246	26,115	0.663	0.685
1947	44,464	641	2,883	16,076	0.420	0.441
1948	62,150	1,424	4,511	8,329	0.202	0.230
1949	62,792	1,685	4,583	21,000	0.397	0.434
1950	69,571	2,708	5,814	39,482	0.627	0.690
1951	68,022	2,133	5,824	32,513	0.546	0.595
1952	66,010	5,075	5,300	31,583	0.519	0.636
1953	70,285	6,964	5,589	24,297	0.387	0.524
1954	72,983	10,599	6,875	120,278	1.521	1.887
1955	81,950	27,056	8,520	87,516	0.881	1.502
1956	86,675	34,611	9,445	87,703	0.801	1.520
1957	87,355	30,747	9,657	101,716	0.943	1.627
1958	80,376	16,555	10,892	214,220	2.322	3.007
1959	83,449	33,383	11,518	136,188	1.264	2.170
1960	82,172	36,811	12,173	181,309	1.626	2.803
1961	81,272	34,371	12,341	231,646	2.110	3.425
1962	83,489	37,140	14,743	171,248	1.542	2.673
1963	82,060	23,797	15,492	148,349	1.548	2.287
Average:						
1940–44	$42,810	$ 1,217	$ 4,511	$ 28,492	0.750	0.799
1960–63	82.248	33,030	13,687	183,138	1.707	2.795

rise substantially, at least in the later years depicted. From 1960 through 1963, dividends, capital gains, and stock-connected compensation items together outweighed nonownership income by almost three-to-one in the totals.

Either set of revised figures, therefore, reconfirms the view that the bulk of annual managerial income attributable to employer companies emanates from sources whose exploitation by management is consistent with the advancement of shareholder interests. While we could engage in a more exhaustive range of similiar—perhaps progressively more detailed—"sensitivity" tests, it does not seem useful to belabor the point, given the pattern of results we can see developing.[11] Ownership-related income elements turn out, under a wide range of computational approaches, to provide anywhere from two out of every three to six out of every seven dollars' worth of observable increments to personal wealth experienced in recent years by the senior executives of large, publicly held manufacturing corporations.[12] The inference here is that this circumstance augurs well for the kind of active congruence of management and stockholder objectives on which the profit-maximizing hypothesis of conventional economic models depends.[13]

Executive Ownership Proportions

The prevailing belief that professional managers have become increasingly *less* involved in ownership over time does, however, have a degree of empirical backing which merits our attention. It happens, as Table 25 documents, that the *fraction* of his employer firm's common stock which the typical highly paid corporate officer owned indeed declined between 1940 and 1963, even though the associated annual income flows sharply increased. Thus, on January 1, 1940,

[11] We could also reexamine these new comparisons by stipulating a 25 per cent effective capital gains tax rate and a higher taxable outside income assumption. Neither analysis would, as they did not before, have much impact on the findings.

[12] The holdings by executives of shares in corporations other than their employer's have not, of course, been included in these comparisons for lack of the requisite data. This issue will be addressed in Chapter 7.

[13] Or, equivalently, share-price-maximizing. See the discussion in Chapter 1.

TABLE 25

Trends in Proportionate Ownership:
Large Manufacturing Sample, 1940–63

	1940	1963
Full Sample		
Mean per capita stockholdings:		
Top executives	$682,502	$2,624,557
Top five executives	$574,743	$2,365,847
Implied total holdings:		
50 top executives	$34,125,100	$131,227,850
250 top five executives	$143,685,750	$591,461,750
Total market value of the 50 sample		
corporations	$13,585,895,000	$101,077,471,000
Fraction of total owned by executives:		
Top executives	0.2512%	0.1298%
Top five executives	1.0576%	0.5852%
Reduced Sample with		
Extreme Values Deleted		
Mean per capita stockholdings:		
Top executive	$458,756	$1,152,847
Top five executives	$269,857	$861,286
Implied total holdings:		
50 top executives	$22,937,800	$57,642,350
250 top five executives	$67,464,250	$215,321,500
Total market value of the 50 sample		
corporations	$13,585,895,000	$101,077,471,000
Fraction of total owned by executives:		
Top executives	0.1688%	0.0570%
Top five executives	0.5703%	0.2130%

the mean per capita stockholdings of the respective chief executives of the fifty companies in the sample were $682,502 in market value terms. The total holdings for fifty such individuals would therefore have amounted to $34,125,100. This latter figure represented just over one-quarter of 1 per cent of the aggregate market value of all fifty corporations' outstanding common shares on January 1, 1940. By January 1, 1963, the per capita top executive equity investment had risen to $2,624,557, but the combined market value of the sample companies had risen at a sufficiently more rapid pace so that those higher individual holdings came to only about one-eighth of 1 per cent of the corporate total, indicating a reduction of roughly one-half in the proportionate ownership shares under consideration.

Data for the top five executives together—which show a somewhat milder secular decrease in percentage ownership—are also presented in the table, as are comparisons for both executive categories using the per capita stockholdings implied by the deletion of extreme individual values. Whatever the focus, there is no doubt that the relative size of senior management's holdings did, in fact, diminish during the quarter-century period studied. Evidence of this sort would appear to be the genesis of the concern that executives may have become progressively less sensitive to shareholder aspirations over the years.

The contention here is that this interpretation misses the point. The issue is not how much of his company a professional manager owns; the issue is how important that portfolio is in relation to his *personal* income opportunities. Ownership positions on the order of one-tenth of 1 per cent may seem trivial as judged by the voting power they confer at an annual shareholders' meeting, but ownership positions of $2.5 million which can produce capital gains and dividends amounting to $500,000 yearly do not seem trivial in the context of a compensation package totaling only $200,000, half of which is itself stock-price dependent. Because the market value and the income consequences of top executives' equity investments in their own firms have grown at a substantially faster historical rate than their non-ownership sources of reward as employees, the net result, as seen here, is a marked *gain,* rather than a loss, in ownership income sensitivity at the individual managerial level. As long as that phenomenon persists, the proportionate ownership fractions involved—while perhaps intriguing to identify—are analytically redundant and very likely misleading as well.

Portfolio Activity

The argument was made earlier that, in specifying an effective tax rate on executives' capital gains from holdings of their firms' stock, we could assume such gains to be primarily long-term in nature. The stock ownership data on which the analysis of the current chapter is based substantiate that claim. An examination of the 5,241 separate man-years of compensation and shareholding experience which comprise the full large-manufacturing sample indicates that in only 2,269 of those intervals—approximately 43 per cent—was there *any* trading at all by the executive in his employer's securities during the year. Moreover, in 1,453 of these situations, the trades observed involved net *additions* to holdings within the year, leaving just 816 instances in which a net sale of shares occurred.[14] This represents a mere 16 per cent of the total number of man-years at issue between 1940 and 1963.[15] That degree of turnover in top management's portfolio clearly fails to support the view that executives are doing much manipulating of their firms' stock, or that they are profiteering very heavily in response to inside information. It also suggests that the great majority of trades which take place necessarily satisfy the waiting period requirements for capital gains tax treatment.[16] Thus, senior manufacturing officers do not, in fact, revise their holdings very frequently; in particular, they do not sell very often; and the secular declines we find in percentage ownership of employer-company stock must, therefore, result from the replacement of retiring executives by successors whose holdings are somewhat smaller

[14] In making these calculations, of course, the impact of stock splits and stock dividends was considered. A man whose holdings rose from 1,000 shares to 1,050 shares in the course of a year wherein a 5 per cent stock dividend was paid by his company was, for example, not counted as having experienced a change in ownership.

[15] The proportionate number of *individuals* who sold shares on balance during their careers is almost exactly the same. Only 90 out of the 552 on the list, or again 16 per cent, left the sample—i.e., died, retired, or resigned—owning fewer shares than when they entered it.

[16] The SEC strictures on short-term trading profits by corporate directors, and the consequent vulnerability of such profits to shareholder legal action, undoubtedly have played a part in discouraging rapid turnover.

to begin with, rather than from a liquidation of holdings over time by given individuals.[17]

Summary

The investments by the top executives of large, publicly held industrial enterprises in the common shares of their own firms are much more substantial than is generally supposed, running to more than $2 million per capita in recent years. The significance of those investments is perhaps best measured by the predominance of the attendant capital gains and dividends in the aggregate income profile of the men in question—a finding which is reinforced by the evidence that a sizeable fraction of employee remuneration is itself attributable to stock-related pay schemes. An investigation of the historical relationships involved reveals that this phenomenon has become progressively stronger since 1940, surmounting a trend toward a rather lower *relative* level of participation in ownership by top management, as judged by the proportionate share of total company common stock owned. The modest secular rate of increase in executive compensation, coupled with steadily higher dividend payments and an exuberant securities market, accounts for these observations.

While certain of the conclusions offered depend for their precise dimensions on the set of environmental parameters chosen for the requisite computations, tests of alternative choices and alternative procedures have been seen not to alter the thrust of the analysis. The corporations included in the sample under examination are representative of the class of enterprises for which concern is most frequently expressed regarding the separation of management and

---

[17] Whatever the incentives or pressures not to trade, the one-year-in-six frequency of share liquidation we observe implies that the effective capital gains tax rate of 15 per cent assumed here may indeed be a bit high. The Brookings Institution study cited earlier (Bailey, *op. cit.*) estimated that a four-year holding period is typical of the mass of investors, and that an 8 to 9 per cent effective capital gains tax rate would be indicated by such a turnover pattern. Since executives apparently trade even less often, the effective tax rate for them may well be still lower than Bailey's figure. If so, it would mean that the size of management's after-tax ownership income has been noticeably understated here.

shareholders, and its effect on company direction. The data described do not, of course, completely nullify that concern. They do, however, establish the existence and strength of an income link which has not been adequately recognized or appreciated, and which does offer some support for the traditional model of the firm.

5

STOCK OWNERSHIP AND INCOME:
RETAIL TRADE

GIVEN THE SETTING provided by the preceding evidence on ownership and compensation in large manufacturing companies, we may turn to a determination of the extent to which the conclusions indicated hold more generally for the business community. In particular, do the organizational differences, the singular historical patterns of development, and the distinctive operating characteristics of leading retailing enterprises contribute to a management-shareholder relationship which departs markedly from the picture which emerges among industrial firms? The sample to which this question is addressed consists of the fifteen large department and discount-store chains whose executive pay packages were examined earlier. Since the relevance of most of the ownership items with which we shall be concerned has already been established by our discussion to this point, it should be possible to compress the subsequent presentation to a considerable degree.

Stockholdings

As of January 1 of each year from 1940 through 1963, the employer-company common stockholdings of the senior officers of the fifteen corporations at issue were as listed in Table 26 and as depicted in Chart 13. The numbers denote mean values for the sample in all cases and are measured at market price. We see that, in the early 1940's, per capita holdings were in the range of $500,000 to $600,-000 for the highest-paid individual in each firm, and $200,000 to $300,000 for the five highest-paid as a group. By the 1960's, the former figure had increased only slightly—and, indeed, was well

TABLE 26

Average Market Value of Executive Stockholdings:
Retail Trade Sample, 1940–63
(amounts in dollars)

Year	Top Executive	Top Five Executives
1940	682,121	308,917
1941	546,040	271,878
1942	525,693	197,505
1943	549,970	229,222
1944	666,734	283,210
1945	651,901	349,097
1946	1,067,469	630,748
1947	637,296	447,566
1948	515,023	369,823
1949	556,803	337,515
1950	876,697	369,948
1951	739,583	461,641
1952	660,559	402,539
1953	462,122	302,093
1954	374,423	292,937
1955	857,898	314,931
1956	545,348	256,838
1957	847,540	346,640
1958	299,159	266,883
1959	519,147	488,877
1960	531,576	567,957
1961	441,603	599,249
1962	692,110	823,669
1963	662,424	864,517

CHART 13

MARKET VALUE OF EXECUTIVE STOCKHOLDINGS: RETAIL TRADE SAMPLE, 1940–63

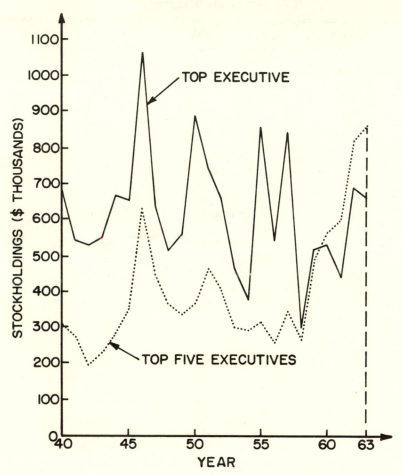

below its peak—while the top-five average had better than doubled.[1] It turns out that much of this eccentricity in the time series can be traced to two or three individuals with unusually extensive holdings, as will soon become evident. Because there is a maximum of just fifteen observations at every executive position each year in the cur-

[1] Once again, preferred stockholdings are omitted from consideration.

rent calculations, a few extreme values can have a greater impact than was true of the fifty company manufacturing data. Even in their present form, however, the tabulations make it clear that retailing executives' equity investments in their own companies have not kept pace with those of their industrial counterparts.[2] The per capita holdings of both samples started at essentially the same level in 1940, but by 1963 the retail trade contingent owned stock worth only one-fourth to one-third as much as that held by men occupying similar administrative positions in manufacturing.

Dividends

The pattern of dividend receipts which accompanied the holdings reflects the same historical relationship. Table 27 records the before-tax and after-tax annual magnitudes for the retailing sample. Dividend income for these men, especially in after-tax terms, matched or exceeded the corresponding manufacturing amounts well into the 1950's, but dropped noticeably behind by the early 1960's. In fact, an *absolute* decline in the dividends claimed each year by the highest-paid executives in retailing occurred between 1940 and 1963. The figures for the five highest-paid men combined were up by roughly one-half. Despite this unimpressive result, the attendant ratio of dividend payments to salary and bonus receipts is still reasonably high, since annual direct cash compensation for the retail group was somewhat below the observed industrial corporation scale.[3] Table 28 indicates that dividends came to approximately 30 per cent of top executive salary-plus-bonus earnings in the early 1940's, and 10 to 15 per cent during the early 1960's. For the top five positions together, the range was from 20 to 25 per cent virtually throughout. Both sets of computations imply that employer-company dividend payments did constitute an important income source over the interval studied.

[2] Table 13 and Chart 11 depict this situation.
[3] This phenomenon also accounts for the smaller effective personal income tax rate on retailing dividend income. Thus, senior retail executives were generally in lower marginal tax brackets than the men on the manufacturing list.

TABLE 27

Average Dividend Receipts: Retail Trade Sample, 1940–63
(amounts in dollars)

	Top Executive		Top Five Executives	
Year	Before Taxes	After Taxes	Before Taxes	After Taxes
1940	32,233	20,685	16,249	10,970
1941	28,243	14,422	15,953	8,585
1942	32,807	14,358	13,210	5,999
1943	36,876	14,084	15,804	6,247
1944	35,252	13,574	16,208	6,245
1945	28,525	10,730	16,331	6,251
1946	38,877	15,873	21,879	9,242
1947	36,013	14,927	27,536	11,568
1948	32,488	18,552	26,198	14,917
1949	35,442	20,362	23,225	13,217
1950	53,672	30,350	23,463	13,255
1951	41,804	23,194	23,997	13,031
1952	36,125	18,964	22,729	11,613
1953	23,341	11,965	15,179	7,731
1954	22,349	12,214	17,496	9,377
1955	47,715	25,550	16,943	9,116
1956	27,730	14,558	12,899	6,851
1957	52,157	27,795	20,140	10,797
1958	17,569	8,519	15,345	8,090
1959	19,791	10,028	20,203	10,730
1960	20,808	10,729	22,358	11,944
1961	15,142	7,385	21,499	11,482
1962	17,815	8,948	23,233	12,337
1963	19,934	9,567	28,135	14,971

TABLE 28

Mean Before-Tax Dividend Receipts as a Per Cent of Mean
Before-Tax Salary Plus Bonus: Retail Trade Sample,
1940–63

Year	Top Executive	Top Five Executives
1940	35	25
1941	25	21
1942	30	17
1943	33	20
1944	30	20
1945	25	20
1946	29	23
1947	29	29
1948	26	27
1949	30	26
1950	44	24
1951	36	26
1952	31	25
1953	20	17
1954	19	19
1955	35	17
1956	20	13
1957	38	20
1958	13	15
1959	14	19
1960	15	22
1961	11	21
1962	12	22
1963	14	26

Capital Gains

A still more important source were the increments to personal wealth associated with the market price changes in executives' shareholdings. Table 29 summarizes the mean annual capital gains and losses experienced by the individuals in question. It appears that although the figures do not quite compare in size with those confronted by manufacturing executives, they are no less volatile from year to year. Indeed, there are, if anything, a *greater* number of sharp and sudden swings from positive to negative values in these tabulations. Chart 14 highlights this circumstance for both the top, and top-five, retail trade officer groups. The transformation of the gains depicted into their absolute-value counterparts—to eliminate the effect on the averages of any offsetting intercorporate market price changes—produces the time series shown in Table 30. As was true of the manufacturing sample, the mean absolute gains here are only marginally larger than the net figures, reflecting the unsurprising tendency of share prices among firms in a given sector of the economy to move together in response to external developments. Once again, of course, the definition of capital gains and losses for each man encompasses accrued as well as realized amounts, and the after-tax magnitudes are calculated using 15 per cent as the assumed effective gains tax rate.

Compensation and Ownership Income

When the dividend receipts and absolute capital gains listed are combined with executives' fixed-dollar and stock-based earnings as employees, the comparisons recorded in Tables 31 and 32 are produced. After-tax ownership income was a little better than twice as large as total after-tax compensation for the highest-paid retail executive category in the early years of the investigation (column 5 of Table 31). Rising levels of reward thereafter, coupled with stagnation in stockholdings, lowered this ratio to just about one-to-one by the 1960's. These findings are, in terms of the orders of magnitude involved, almost exactly the reverse of the corresponding historical manufacturing evidence (Table 18). Over the same period,

TABLE 29

Average Capital Gains: Retail Trade Sample, 1940–63
(amounts in dollars)

	Top Executive		Top Five Executives	
Year	Before Taxes	After Taxes	Before Taxes	After Taxes
1940	−91,004	−77,353	−27,570	−23,434
1941	−98,050	−83,342	−51,869	−44,088
1942	61,997	52,697	16,684	14,181
1943	189,607	161,165	71,629	60,884
1944	122,918	104,479	74,591	63,402
1945	394,524	335,345	303,264	257,774
1946	−182,364	−155,009	−112,988	−96,039
1947	−85,183	−72,405	−60,646	−51,549
1948	−4,737	−4,026	−21,189	−18,010
1949	64,392	54,732	34,752	29,539
1950	188,684	160,382	111,739	94,978
1951	−50,890	−43,257	−46,432	−39,467
1952	−3,431	−2,917	2,333	1,983
1953	−22,874	−19,443	−16,629	−14,134
1954	136,695	116,191	93,623	79,579
1955	107,782	91,691	45,627	38,783
1956	−71,370	−60,664	−33,368	−28,362
1957	−9,604	−8,163	2,498	2,124
1958	171,615	145,873	166,279	141,336
1959	36,856	31,327	102,239	86,903
1960	94,761	80,547	55,343	47,041
1961	194,358	165,204	253,380	215,372
1962	−62,451	−53,083	−105,347	−89,545
1963	155,430	132,115	156,940	133,399

CHART 14

AVERAGE ANNUAL AFTER-TAX CAPITAL GAINS:
RETAIL TRADE SAMPLE, 1940-63

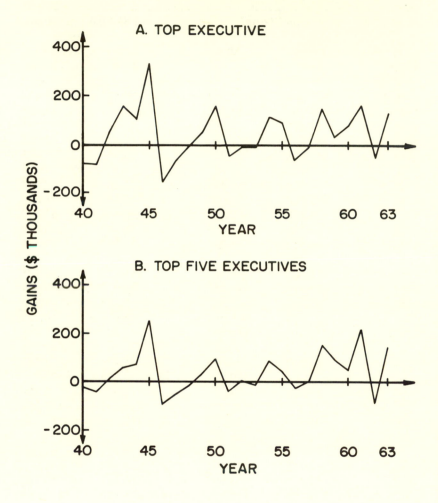

TABLE 30

Average Absolute Capital Gains: Retail Trade Sample, 1940–63
(amounts in dollars)

Year	Top Executive		Top Five Executives	
	Before Taxes	After Taxes	Before Taxes	After Taxes
1940	103,916	88,328	33,635	28,590
1941	99,094	84,230	52,191	44,362
1942	90,864	77,234	27,688	23,534
1943	189,607	161,165	71,629	60,884
1944	122,918	104,479	74,591	63,402
1945	394,524	335,345	303,264	257,774
1946	190,476	161,904	115,456	98,137
1947	86,140	73,218	62,493	53,119
1948	40,240	34,204	46,554	39,570
1949	69,692	59,237	47,691	40,537
1950	223,722	190,164	121,790	103,521
1951	67,022	56,968	55,246	46,958
1952	41,524	35,295	33,110	28,143
1953	25,955	22,061	20,542	17,461
1954	136,847	116,319	93,914	79,826
1955	111,350	94,647	48,211	40,979
1956	71,464	60,744	33,665	28,615
1957	28,304	24,058	16,736	14,226
1958	171,615	145,873	166,279	141,336
1959	37,846	32,169	103,436	87,920
1960	106,358	90,404	59,975	50,978
1961	194,358	165,204	253,380	215,372
1962	74,293	63,149	111,398	94,688
1963	155,826	132,452	157,189	133,610

TABLE 31

Compensation and Ownership Income:
Retail Trade Sample, 1940–63;
Average for the Top Executive in Each Firm

	Compensation		Ownership Income		Comparison	
	(1)	(2)	(3)	(4)	(5)	(6)
	After-	After-				
	Tax	Tax		Absolute		
	Fixed-	Stock-	After-	After-		
	Dollar	Based	Tax	Tax		
	Remu-	Remu-	Dividend	Capital	[(3)+(4)]	[(2)+(3)+(4)]
Year	neration	neration	Income	Gains	[(1)+(2)]	(1)
1940	$ 58,718	$ 430	$ 20,685	$ 88,328	1.843	1.863
1941	56,587	751	14,422	84,230	1.720	1.756
1942	48,409	193	14,358	77,234	1.884	1.896
1943	49,557	152	14,084	161,165	3.525	3.539
1944	55,803	1,173	13,574	104,479	2.071	2.136
1945	43,239	1,165	10,730	335,345	7.793	8.030
1946	57,842	4,915	15,873	161,904	2.832	3.158
1947	59,424	306	14,927	73,218	1.475	1.488
1948	78,247	1,529	18,552	34,204	0.661	0.693
1949	94,550	493	20,362	59,237	0.837	0.847
1950	74,482	1,180	30,350	190,164	2.914	2.976
1951	70,892	901	23,194	56,968	1.116	1.143
1952	67,434	1,218	18,964	35,295	0.790	0.822
1953	68,688	1,722	11,965	22,061	0.483	0.520
1954	91,791	4,248	12,214	116,319	1.338	1.446
1955	80,049	10,531	25,550	94,647	1.326	1.633
1956	87,584	10,740	14,558	60,744	0.765	0.982
1957	94,292	15,022	27,795	24,058	0.474	0.709
1958	91,683	25,831	8,519	145,873	1.313	1.965
1959	89,253	38,838	10,028	32,169	0.329	0.907
1960	81,194	35,319	10,729	90,404	0.867	1.680
1961	79,338	57,279	7,385	165,204	1.263	2.897
1962	80,726	52,730	8,948	63,149	0.540	1.546
1963	87,222	40,068	9,567	132,452	1.115	2.087
Average:						
1940–44	$53,814	$ 540	$15,425	$103,087	2.180	2.212
1960–63	82,120	46,349	9,157	112,802	0.949	2.050

TABLE 32

Compensation and Ownership Income:
Retail Trade Sample, 1940–63;
Average for the Top Five Executives in Each Firm

Year	Compensation		Ownership Income		Comparison	
	(1) After-Tax Fixed-Dollar Remuneration	(2) After-Tax Stock-Based Remuneration	(3) After-Tax Dividend Income	(4) Absolute After-Tax Capital Gains	(5) $\frac{[(3)+(4)]}{[(1)+(2)]}$	(6) $\frac{[(2)+(3)+(4)]}{(1)}$
1940	$45,080	$ 223	$10,970	$ 28,589	0.873	0.882
1941	41,510	258	8,584	44,362	1.267	1.281
1942	37,407	89	5,999	23,534	0.787	0.791
1943	36,708	175	6,246	60,884	1.820	1.833
1944	38,041	409	6,245	63,401	1.811	1.841
1945	35,248	513	6,250	257,774	7.382	7.504
1946	44,099	1,362	9,241	98,136	2.361	2.465
1947	45,430	154	11,567	53,118	1.419	1.427
1948	60,329	535	14,916	39,570	0.895	0.912
1949	65,675	328	13,216	40,536	0.814	0.823
1950	60,994	585	13,254	103,520	1.896	1.924
1951	57,582	543	13,031	46,958	1.032	1.051
1952	54,628	777	11,613	28,142	0.717	0.741
1953	55,213	1,108	7,731	17,460	0.447	0.476
1954	65,232	2,700	9,376	79,826	1.313	1.408
1955	61,905	6,873	9,115	40,979	0.728	0.920
1956	64,678	7,061	6,851	28,615	0.494	0.657
1957	69,822	9,011	10,797	14,225	0.317	0.487
1958	67,384	14,244	8,090	141,336	1.830	2.428
1959	67,724	20,959	10,730	87,920	1.112	1.766
1960	65,752	18,941	11,944	50,978	0.742	1.245
1961	65,599	28,628	11,482	215,372	2.407	3.894
1962	67,520	24,756	12,336	94,687	1.159	1.951
1963	69,346	25,833	14,970	133,609	1.561	2.515
Average:						
1940–44	$39,749	$ 231	$ 7,609	$ 44,154	1.295	1.308
1960–63	67,054	24,540	12,683	123,662	1.489	2.399

the five-highest-paid retailing category enjoyed a slight increase in the ownership fraction of aggregate income, the capital gain and dividend figures growing from 130 per cent to 150 per cent of employee remuneration (column 5, Table 32). The contemporaries of these men in manufacturing, on the other hand, experienced consistently higher ratios both at the beginning and at the end of the relevant interval (Table 19).

The parallel in column 6 of the tabulations for the sum of dividends, capital gains, and stock-based rewards in relation to fixed-dollar earnings yields generally similar results. Ownership and ownership-dependent items are nowhere as overwhelming for the retail manager sample as they were for the matching industrial group, running from two to two-and-one-half times fixed-dollar inflows subsequent to 1960, rather than six to eight times, as was the situation in manufacturing. Such observations, nonetheless, look pale only by comparison. The fact that in recent times more than two out of every three dollars of the increments we can identify to senior managerial personal net worth in large retailing organizations have had an underlying common stock origin, implies that the income exposure of these men to the vagaries of ownership far outweighs their exposure as hired hands. In that respect, the current findings clearly reinforce the manufacturing data.

Sensitivity to Extreme Values

While we could again engage in a test of the response of the results to changes in computational parameters similar to that undertaken in the preceding chapter, the outcome is sufficiently predictable as to obviate the need for such an exercise. An increase in the assumed effective capital gains tax rate would diminish somewhat the apparent role of ownership returns in the totals, and a higher taxable income estimate would have the reverse impact. Taken together, the revisions would be approximately offsetting, as we concluded earlier.

A more useful analysis concerns the extent to which any extreme compensation or stockholding experiences by certain individuals in the sample may distort the averages which have been presented. For that purpose, we may recast the data by removing from the group any executive whose equity investment in his company exceeds by two standard deviations or more the means listed in Table 26 for his position in the retail managerial hierarchy each year. When this is done, and revised means are calculated from the remaining observations, the new stockholding time series of Table 33 emerge. The sample now consists of 1,630 man-years of data—a reduction of approximately 7 per cent from the original 1,757 and a proportionate decline which compares closely with that recorded in manufacturing upon application of a similar criterion for exclusion of unusual cases. In effect, one executive has been removed at virtually every level every year in the present computations, owing to the extraordinary nature of his personal portfolio.[4] As before, all the deletions occur at the upper end of the various distributions.

The modified market value averages are generally one-half to two-thirds the size of the full-sample means from Table 26. The secular trend, however, is changed very little. The typical top retail executive's employer-company equity investments were slightly higher in the early 1960's than they were in the early 1940's, while the figures for the top-five category roughly doubled over the same span. Since the latter started from a lower base, we find that the stockholding gradient across the five positions has diminished considerably within the quarter-century period studied. The deletions also reduce the volatility of the year-to-year market values of the relevant holdings, a phenomenon which was discernible previously in the manufacturing data. The net result is a historical record which still shows sizeable per capita common stockholdings, but which, like the full-sample evidence, portrays a rather more modest level of ownership involvement among senior retail officers than prevails in large industrial firms. The associated dividends and capital gains are listed in Appendix E, a similar diminution in the figures of one-third to one-half, as compared with the original averages, manifesting itself.

---

[4] Thus, there are 127 exclusions in all out of an array of 120 possible locations—5 positions over 24 years.

TABLE 33

Average Market Value of Executive Stockholdings:
Retail Trade Sample, 1940–63; Extreme Values Deleted
(amounts in dollars)

Year	Top Executive	Top Five Executives
1940	480,011	204,532
1941	398,447	181,736
1942	427,111	145,625
1943	398,727	154,125
1944	481,542	171,653
1945	452,410	208,930
1946	736,403	288,435
1947	379,743	206,134
1948	304,795	171,969
1949	341,716	152,943
1950	673,250	205,310
1951	468,920	216,476
1952	413,998	164,058
1953	211,915	129,492
1954	131,012	143,082
1955	523,278	193,465
1956	324,760	164,703
1957	392,751	178,620
1958	212,632	147,752
1959	368,451	214,366
1960	385,836	266,845
1961	340,645	277,245
1962	572,768	363,251
1963	532,654	400,046

Relationship to Compensation

The real issue, of course, is not simply the magnitude of the reductions occasioned by removing extreme values, but the impact of such an operation on the implied relative importance of ownership and ownership-dependent items in the aggregate managerial income structure. For that comparison, extraordinary compensation experiences in retailing were also identified and deleted by using a 2σ test on the distribution of total after-tax earnings at each of the five positions each year. The consequence for average total compensation is depicted in the Appendix. The sample on which these revised means are based contains 1,671 observations, suggesting a pattern of dispersion in the executive pay figures of somewhat smaller dimensions than in the concurrent stockholdings. When the new compensation totals are separated into their fixed-dollar and stock-related components, and combined with the after-tax dividend and absolute capital gains averages just computed, the relationships summarized in Tables 34 and 35 emerge.

According to those data, the typical chief executive in retailing enjoyed, during the early years of the study, capital gains and dividends which amounted to 171 per cent of his aggregate employee remuneration. At the same time, capital gains, dividends, and stock-based pay together came to 173 per cent of fixed-dollar compensation. By the 1960's, the corresponding ratios had fallen to 83 and 159 per cent, respectively. A decline over the years in the role of ownership returns is therefore still apparent. Annual dividends and capital gains for the five highest-paid officers as a group held fairly steady at about three-fourths of total pay during the entire period, while the sum of those items plus stock-related earnings of various kinds approximately matched fixed-dollar receipts throughout. (The relevant comparison is with the manufacturing sample time series in Tables 23 and 24.) The fact that the ownership segment of retail trade executives' income turns out by all these standards to be noticeably smaller than that revealed by our examination of large industrial corporations is obviously attributable both to the lower per capita levels of stock ownership and to the lesser emphasis on stock-connected forms of

TABLE 34

Compensation and Ownership Income:
Retail Trade Sample, 1940–63;
Average for the Top Executive in Each Firm,
Extreme Values Deleted

Year	Compensation		Ownership Income		Comparison	
	(1) After-Tax Fixed-Dollar Remuneration	(2) After-Tax Stock-Based Remuneration	(3) After-Tax Dividend Income	(4) Absolute After-Tax Capital Gains	(5) $\frac{[(3)+(4)]}{[(1)+(2)]}$	(6) $\frac{[(2)+(3)+(4)]}{(1)}$
1940	$54,634	$ 461	$13,750	$ 32,299	0.835	0.851
1941	52,703	809	10,190	55,148	1.220	1.255
1942	44,002	207	11,358	45,292	1.281	1.292
1943	41,403	178	11,437	136,600	3.560	3.579
1944	47,491	0	10,912	86,751	2.056	2.056
1945	43,239	1,165	7,924	244,933	5.694	5.874
1946	58,816	0	12,785	98,564	1.893	1.893
1947	56,156	328	9,943	41,895	0.917	0.928
1948	74,867	1,639	11,857	28,635	0.529	0.562
1949	73,719	529	13,855	52,523	0.894	0.907
1950	74,482	1,180	24,590	153,321	2.351	2.404
1951	68,056	965	14,746	36,967	0.749	0.774
1952	64,590	1,305	13,277	29,986	0.656	0.690
1953	65,933	1,456	5,826	15,367	0.314	0.343
1954	71,132	3,759	4,454	35,342	0.531	0.612
1955	77,305	7,291	14,962	79,789	1.120	1.319
1956	87,584	10,740	9,506	28,883	0.390	0.560
1957	87,852	4,698	11,646	25,777	0.404	0.479
1958	91,009	17,417	6,380	83,502	0.828	1.178
1959	87,103	27,969	7,479	34,275	0.362	0.800
1960	82,556	25,302	8,083	57,213	0.605	1.097
1961	78,206	47,324	6,039	136,945	1.139	2.433
1962	82,054	33,513	7,981	66,235	0.642	1.312
1963	84,050	28,868	8,513	92,273	0.892	1.542
Averages:						
1940–44	$48,047	$ 331	$11,529	$ 71,218	1.710	1.729
1960–63	81,717	33,752	7,654	88,167	0.830	1.586

TABLE 35

Compensation and Ownership Income:
Retail Trade Sample, 1940–63;
Average for the Top Five Executives in Each Firm,
Extreme Values Deleted

Year	Compensation		Ownership Income		Comparison	
	(1) After- Tax Fixed- Dollar Remu- neration	(2) After- Tax Stock- Based Remu- neration	(3) After- Tax Dividend Income	(4) Absolute After- Tax Capital Gains	(5) $\frac{[(3)+(4)]}{[(1)+(2)]}$	(6) $\frac{[(2)+(3)+(4)]}{(1)}$
1940	$45,558	$ 237	$7,031	$ 12,942	0.436	0.443
1941	42,203	278	5,620	26,466	0.755	0.766
1942	36,593	95	4,352	13,921	0.498	0.501
1943	33,897	197	4,584	45,464	1.467	1.482
1944	36,500	186	3,909	30,637	0.941	0.951
1945	35,450	518	3,968	107,818	3.107	3.168
1946	43,125	401	5,129	40,590	1.050	1.069
1947	43,883	164	5,225	19,548	0.562	0.568
1948	60,066	563	6,386	14,501	0.344	0.357
1949	57,364	346	6,207	22,407	0.495	0.504
1950	60,994	585	7,581	44,514	0.845	0.863
1951	56,962	573	6,617	15,007	0.375	0.389
1952	54,059	795	5,208	10,446	0.285	0.304
1953	54,662	1,055	3,986	9,286	0.238	0.262
1954	59,026	2,342	5,112	38,847	0.716	0.784
1955	61,356	6,225	5,696	27,051	0.484	0.635
1956	64,678	7,061	4,822	16,599	0.298	0.440
1957	67,803	6,999	5,462	9,671	0.202	0.326
1958	67,605	7,759	4,571	58,499	0.836	1.047
1959	67,614	15,177	4,895	24,205	0.351	0.654
1960	65,774	14,958	5,484	34,290	0.492	0.832
1961	65,409	19,191	5,276	85,149	1.068	1.675
1962	67,810	17,650	5,626	37,721	0.507	0.899
1963	68,953	14,047	6,251	69,889	0.917	1.307
Average:						
1940–44	$38,950	$ 199	$5,099	$ 25,886	0.791	0.801
1960–63	66,987	16,462	5,659	56,762	0.748	1.178

compensation in retailing enterprises.[5] The contention here remains, however, that the degree of effective employer-company ownership involvement apparent for senior retail management is sufficiently impressive to suggest a strong and continuing sensitivity to shareholder interests.

Ownership Fractions

Even though retailing executives' equity investments in their firms, on an individual basis, fall short of the scale characteristic of their industrial counterparts, it happens that the investments we do observe have been somewhat more important in terms of the total outstanding common stock of the corporations in question. Table 36 shows that the top executive category in the 15 retailing companies owned shares accounting for roughly one-half of 1 per cent of the aggregate market value of those companies just prior to World War II— regardless of whether the full-sample, or reduced-sample, mean is taken to be the appropriate criterion. The proportions for the top-five executive group were in the neighborhood of 1 per cent. By 1963, the combined holdings of top executives had diminished to less than one-tenth of 1 per cent of the then-larger total market value of their firms, while the top-five average was in the range of three-tenths to six-tenths of a per cent, depending upon the standard chosen. With the exception of the 1963 top executive figure, all these fractions substantially exceed those recorded earlier for manufacturing (see Table 25). As judged by the voting power they connote, of course, they are all also rather trivial—but it is the relationship between the attendant dividends and capital gains, and executives' other income components, which should continue to be our concern.

Turnover of the Holdings

A look at the extent to which senior retailing executives trade in their firms' securities confirms the conclusion drawn earlier that there is

[5] With regard to the latter point, see Chapter 3.

TABLE 36

Trends in Proportionate Ownership: Retail Trade Sample, 1940–63

	1940	1963
Full Sample		
Mean per capita stockholdings:		
Top executives	$682,121	$662,424
Top five executives	$308,917	$864,517
Implied total holdings:		
15 top executives	$10,231,815	$9,936,360
75 top five executives	$23,168,775	$64,838,775
Total market value of the 15 sample corporations	$1,742,356,000	$10,382,645,000
Fraction of total owned by executives:		
Top executives	0.5872%	0.0957%
Top five executives	1.3297%	0.6245%
Reduced Sample with Extreme Values Deleted		
Mean per capita stockholdings:		
Top executives	$480,011	$532,654
Top five executives	$204,532	$400,046
Implied total holdings:		
15 top executives	$7,200,165	$7,989,810
75 top five executives	$15,339,900	$30,003,450
Total market value of the 15 sample corporations	$1,742,356,000	$10,382,645,000
Fraction of total owned by executives:		
Top executives	0.4132%	0.0770%
Top five executives	0.8804%	0.2890%

very little short-term activity of the sort which would imply a manipulation of prices for personal advantage or the improper use of inside information. Out of the 1,757 man-years of individual stock ownership experience which comprise the full retail sample data matrix, changes in the number of shares held within a given year [6] by

[6] Excluding, that is, changes occasioned by stock splits and stock dividends.

the men at issue occurred in only 767 instances, or 44 per cent of the total possible opportunities. The comparable figure for the large manufacturing sample was 43 per cent. Since more than half of those trades—395 in all—gave rise to *increases* in executives' holdings, the remaining 372 transactions which had the effect of reducing ownership represent just 21 per cent of the sample observations. In only one year out of five, therefore, do we find these men being net sellers of employer-firm common shares.[7] Once again, the assumption made in the calculations that long-term capital gains tax rates would apply to any profits realized from such transactions seems to be supported.

Summary

An investigation of the participation by the top management of large retailing organizations in the ownership of their own companies reveals holdings on the order of $500,000 to $900,000 per man during the 1960's. The annual capital gains and dividends which resulted either matched or exceeded the total after-tax compensation enjoyed by the same individuals in their professional managerial roles. Indeed, the combination of direct ownership returns of this sort, plus the benefits obtained from common-stock-based instruments of remuneration, have, since 1960, provided two to two-and-one-half times as much income as fixed-dollar rewards. The elimination from the data of both extreme values of compensation and extraordinary levels of ownership modifies the findings to a degree, but they still give evidence of an important and durable link between the economic circumstances of shareholders and the personal wealth of senior executives which belies the notion that no viable mechanism exists for eliciting managerial concern with the interests of the small investor.

[7] The fact that the corresponding rate in large manufacturing companies was but one year out of six may explain in part why per capita stock ownership among executives in those companies grew more rapidly in market value terms over the years than was the case in retailing.

6

STOCK OWNERSHIP AND INCOME: SMALL MANUFACTURERS

WHILE THE PATTERN of employer-company equity investment by the top management of large industrial and retailing firms displays considerable consistency, it is appropriate to inquire whether, and to what extent, that pattern has a counterpart in the context of rather smaller corporations before generalizing too readily about the evidence uncovered. Accordingly, a group of fifteen small to medium-size manufacturing companies comprises the final sample to which attention will be directed. This sample should serve to round out the empirical effort sufficiently to permit some reasonable confidence that any common findings will have broader applicability within the economy.

Stockholdings

The foremost executives of these smaller industrial enterprises owned, as of the start of each calendar year from 1940 to 1963, shares of their firms' common stock having the mean market values listed in Table 37 and portrayed in Chart 15. The data are, in many respects, even more striking than those associated with the two previous samples. The average holdings of the highest-paid men in each of the 15 companies exceeded $2 million in 1940 and had increased to the $3 to $4 million range by the late 1950's and early 1960's. The concomitant rise for the five-highest-paid category was from approximately $600,000 in 1940 to better than $1 million in 1963. Both sets of figures thereby imply a level of personal commitment to ownership by executives which is not only impressive but persistent.

TABLE 37

Average Market Value of Executive Stockholdings: Small Manufacturing Sample, 1940–63
(amounts in dollars)

Year	Top Executive	Top Five Executives
1940	2,732,158	637,434
1941	2,546,068	586,958
1942	1,668,224	424,421
1943	2,716,235	621,457
1944	3,290,842	764,796
1945	3,328,328	782,801
1946	3,918,000	909,648
1947	3,107,535	717,761
1948	2,930,140	657,939
1949	2,928,507	653,021
1950	3,534,511	778,534
1951	3,327,211	743,096
1952	3,253,108	719,054
1953	3,358,447	737,915
1954	3,678,493	780,235
1955	4,193,870	895,258
1956	4,371,845	932,840
1957	4,228,979	934,437
1958	3,650,918	785,483
1959	3,882,826	913,304
1960	2,749,830	786,115
1961	3,265,710	872,480
1962	4,322,911	1,239,810
1963	3,489,437	1,033,769

CHART 15

MARKET VALUE OF EXECUTIVE STOCKHOLDINGS:
SMALL MANUFACTURING SAMPLE, 1940-63

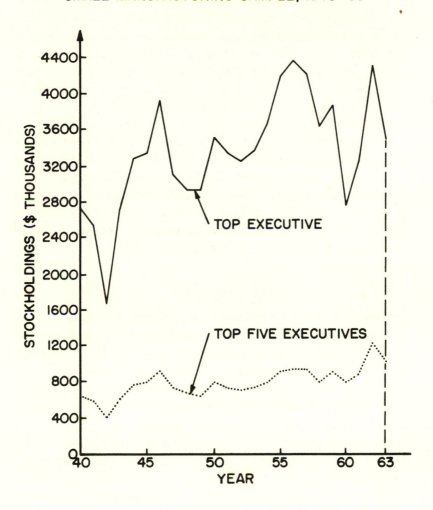

Dividends

Equally impressive is the dividend income which that commitment produces. Table 38 records the relevant mean annual receipts. We observe that the top officer group in small manufacturing corporations enjoyed dividends from employer-company shares amounting generally to between $150,000 and $250,000 before taxes per year during the period studied, while the top-five average was typically in the neighborhood of $40,000 to $50,000. Those payments loom especially large when compared with the other major source of direct cash income—salary and bonus earnings. Table 39 indicates that dividends have surpassed salaries and bonuses by ratios of two-to-one or three-to-one quite consistently at the top executive rank, and have either matched or fallen just short of such compensation in most years for all five senior men combined.[1] Neither the large manufacturing nor the retail trade sample experience suggested anything even approaching a role for dividends of equivalent dimensions.

Capital Gains

The concurrent capital gains—both realized and accrued—are shown in Table 40 and Chart 16. Because of the very sizeable underlying stockholdings, the annual increments to wealth which result from fluctuations in share prices are, of course, substantial. On the average, the highest-paid individuals in the firms at issue were subjected to after-tax capital gains and losses which ran from a low of $150,000 to a peak of almost $1 million per calendar year after 1960. The parallel means for the five-highest-paid men together were in the $30,000 to $300,000 bracket. Sharp reversals in the annual figures from positive to negative are apparent in a number of instances, documenting the same high degree of executive exposure to market contingencies which featured the data for the other two samples.

---

[1] Any concern that payments on this scale may render invalid the taxable income assumption utilized throughout the analysis in estimating tax liabilities on cash income is somewhat premature. As will become evident below, a few extreme stockholding figures strongly influence the means presented and, when those extreme values are set aside, the dividend averages drop precipitously.

TABLE 38

Average Dividend Receipts: Small Manufacturing Sample, 1940–63
(amounts in dollars)

Year	Top Executive		Top Five Executives	
	Before Taxes	After Taxes	Before Taxes	After Taxes
1940	149,203	108,912	34,430	25,547
1941	148,203	87,094	34,423	20,600
1942	113,085	56,251	28,834	14,869
1943	155,536	69,619	36,036	16,519
1944	147,137	65,950	34,511	15,877
1945	139,850	62,705	32,657	14,950
1946	142,139	71,083	33,365	16,913
1947	144,681	71,484	33,899	17,038
1948	183,266	116,389	41,201	26,401
1949	219,131	131,805	48,635	29,644
1950	225,506	140,300	49,601	31,216
1951	205,956	124,329	46,493	28,337
1952	189,680	101,868	42,259	22,921
1953	186,053	99,555	42,161	22,845
1954	183,205	105,606	40,242	23,362
1955	225,397	129,316	48,722	28,172
1956	236,866	134,296	50,793	29,031
1957	210,693	122,143	46,672	27,196
1958	216,684	125,668	46,579	27,181
1959	175,742	102,503	43,027	25,044
1960	147,751	87,510	40,733	24,435
1961	157,367	99,536	42,277	26,492
1962	148,778	96,397	42,620	26,849
1963	146,952	95,154	43,476	27,170

TABLE 39

Mean Before-Tax Dividend Receipts as a Per Cent of Mean Before-Tax Salary Plus Bonus: Small Manufacturing Sample, 1940–63

Year	Top Executive	Top Five Executives
1940	289	113
1941	275	106
1942	205	85
1943	292	111
1944	272	105
1945	258	97
1946	251	88
1947	237	82
1948	275	96
1949	364	117
1950	329	116
1951	298	100
1952	256	86
1953	262	88
1954	261	84
1955	312	98
1956	294	95
1957	280	87
1958	285	87
1959	217	75
1960	188	70
1961	208	74
1962	204	69
1963	180	69

TABLE 40

Average Capital Gains: Small Manufacturing Sample, 1940–63
(amounts in dollars)

	Top Executive		Top Five Executives	
Year	Before Taxes	After Taxes	Before Taxes	After Taxes
1940	−225,023	−191,269	−53,750	−45,688
1941	−689,225	−585,841	−157,041	−133,484
1942	55,392	47,083	21,166	17,991
1943	612,010	520,208	138,635	117,839
1944	171,012	145,360	52,684	44,781
1945	552,911	469,974	140,409	119,347
1946	−754,721	−641,513	−171,281	−145,589
1947	−121,495	−103,271	−23,900	−20,315
1948	90,210	76,679	14,573	12,387
1949	573,331	487,331	123,491	104,967
1950	−186,058	−158,149	−38,229	−32,495
1951	−202,901	−172,465	−37,771	−32,106
1952	53,549	45,517	11,557	9,823
1953	302,282	256,940	58,138	49,418
1954	588,515	500,237	135,505	115,179
1955	40,196	34,166	16,594	14,104
1956	−95,749	−81,387	2,511	2,134
1957	−593,907	−504,821	−141,543	−120,311
1958	538,764	457,949	133,194	113,215
1959	−94,525	−80,346	27,459	23,340
1960	487,714	414,557	100,777	85,660
1961	1,101,600	936,360	320,546	272,464
1962	−680,945	−578,803	−150,847	−128,219
1963	−183,890	−156,307	35,052	29,793

CHART 16

AVERAGE ANNUAL AFTER-TAX CAPITAL GAINS:
SMALL MANUFACTURING SAMPLE, 1940-63

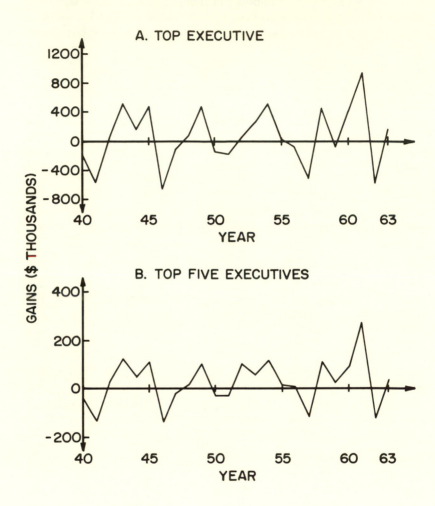

An appreciation for the average absolute changes in wealth generated by these contingencies is provided in Table 41. We see again that the share prices of the fifteen corporations ordinarily moved in similar directions within given intervals, but that there *were* some offsetting interfirm movements which acted to dampen the net gains calculations. Thus, the smallest mean after-tax wealth increment from employer-company shares after 1960 becomes $232,000 for the pertinent top executives and $115,000 for the top five, according to the absolute gains record.[2]

Ownership Income and Compensation

The juxtaposition of those gains, the tabulated after-tax dividends, and the managerial compensation evidence from Chapter 3, produces the comparisons summarized in Tables 42 and 43. Annual capital gains and dividends combined turn out to have been roughly thirteen times as great as aggregate employee remuneration for the chief executives of small industrial enterprises during the early 1940's, and nine times as great during the early 1960's. The corresponding ratios for the five highest-paid men were approximately four and one-half to one and four-to-one, respectively. Since the amounts of stock-based earnings included in the typical pay package among such firms have been rather modest, the relationship of dividends plus gains plus stock compensation to fixed-dollar rewards, as listed in column 6 of the tables, differs little in any year from its counterpart in column 5. Both sets of figures, however, comfortably exceed those applicable to the two preceding samples [3] and, as presented, clearly imply that the ownership component of senior management's annual income is dominant.

Dispersion of the Holdings

On the other hand, the averages for the current sample also happen to be affected much more significantly by a handful of extraordinary

---

[2] The reference is to Tables 16, 17, 29, and 30 for the large manufacturing and retail trade data.

[3] Tables 18, 19, 31, and 32.

TABLE 41

Average Absolute Capital Gains:
Small Manufacturing Sample, 1940–63
(amounts in dollars)

Year	Top Executive		Top Five Executives	
	Before Taxes	After Taxes	Before Taxes	After Taxes
1940	292,799	248,879	67,893	57,708
1941	701,954	596,661	161,171	136,995
1942	75,524	64,195	26,626	22,632
1943	612,010	520,208	138,635	117,839
1944	171,139	145,468	52,761	44,846
1945	552,911	469,974	140,409	119,347
1946	763,663	649,113	174,887	148,654
1947	134,482	114,309	30,036	25,530
1948	190,661	162,061	45,856	38,978
1949	589,533	501,103	128,579	109,292
1950	256,872	218,341	58,067	49,357
1951	215,285	182,991	53,332	45,332
1952	54,994	46,744	13,337	11,336
1953	343,496	291,971	76,543	65,061
1954	588,515	500,237	135,505	115,179
1955	70,966	60,320	25,498	21,673
1956	220,214	187,181	68,472	58,201
1957	597,176	507,599	142,411	121,049
1958	538,764	457,949	133,194	113,215
1959	158,490	134,716	79,414	67,501
1960	527,445	448,328	145,790	123,921
1961	1,106,174	940,247	323,716	275,158
1962	690,132	586,612	196,504	167,028
1963	273,155	232,182	136,137	115,716

TABLE 42

Compensation and Ownership Income:
Small Manufacturing Sample, 1940–63;
Average for the Top Executive in Each Firm

Year	Compensation		Ownership Income		Comparison	
	(1) After-Tax Fixed-Dollar Remu-neration	(2) After-Tax Stock-Based Remu-neration	(3) After-Tax Dividend Income	(4) Absolute After-Tax Capital Gains	(5) $\frac{[(3)+(4)]}{[(1)+(2)]}$	(6) $\frac{[(2)+(3)+(4)]}{(1)}$
1940	$37,682	$ —	$108,912	$248,879	9.495	9.495
1941	32,168	1,033	87,094	596,661	20.594	21.287
1942	28,746	735	56,251	64,195	4.085	4.215
1943	26,030	561	69,619	520,208	22.181	22.681
1944	28,001	—	65,950	145,468	7.550	7.550
1945	26,870	—	62,705	469,974	19.824	19.824
1946	30,877	—	71,083	649,113	23.324	23.324
1947	38,616	—	71,484	114,309	4.811	4.811
1948	46,595	—	116,389	162,061	5.975	5.975
1949	56,915	—	131,805	501,103	11.120	11.120
1950	51,872	—	140,300	218,341	6.913	6.913
1951	49,361	—	124,329	182,991	6.225	6.225
1952	49,323	37	101,868	46,744	3.010	3.013
1953	59,910	441	99,555	291,971	6.487	6.542
1954	65,309	163	105,606	500,237	9.253	9.279
1955	60,972	3,272	129,316	60,320	2.951	3.163
1956	81,355	3,771	134,296	187,181	3.776	3.997
1957	70,581	7,067	122,143	507,599	8.110	9.022
1958	64,311	5,202	125,668	457,949	8.395	9.155
1959	59,800	7,089	102,503	134,716	3.546	4.085
1960	59,258	10,907	87,510	448,328	7.636	9.226
1961	59,905	6,517	99,536	940,247	15.654	17.465
1962	74,496	19,990	96,397	586,612	6.270	8.220
1963	62,017	3,533	95,154	232,182	4.994	5.335
Average:						
1940–44	$30,525	$ 466	$ 77,565	$315,082	12.670	12.878
1960–63	63,919	10,237	94,649	551,842	8.718	10.274

TABLE 43

Compensation and Ownership Income:
Small Manufacturing Sample, 1940–63;
Average for the Top Five Executives in Each Firm

	Compensation		Ownership Income		Comparison	
	(1) After- Tax Fixed- Dollar Remu- neration	(2) After- Tax Stock- Based Remu- neration	(3) After- Tax Dividend Income	(4) Absolute After- Tax Capital Gains	(5) [(3)+(4)] [(1)+(2)]	(6) [(2)+(3)+(4)] (1)
Year						
1940	$24,502	$ —	$25,547	$ 57,708	3.397	3.397
1941	21,854	234	20,600	136,995	7.134	7.221
1942	20,055	171	14,869	22,632	1.854	1.878
1943	17,896	134	16,519	117,839	7.451	7.515
1944	18,991	—	15,877	44,846	3.197	3.197
1945	19,617	—	14,950	119,347	6.845	6.845
1946	22,886	—	16,913	148,654	7.234	7.234
1947	27,161	—	17,038	25,530	1.567	1.567
1948	32,606	—	26,401	38,978	2.005	2.005
1949	34,607	—	29,644	109,292	4.014	4.014
1950	33,728	—	31,216	49,357	2.388	2.388
1951	34,588	—	28,337	45,332	2.129	2.129
1952	34,041	65	22,921	11,336	1.004	1.008
1953	38,057	267	22,845	65,061	2.293	2.316
1954	40,174	50	23,362	115,179	3.444	3.449
1955	40,310	1,544	28,172	21,673	1.190	1.274
1956	47,647	2,087	29,031	58,201	1.753	1.874
1957	44,235	2,026	27,196	121,049	3.204	3.397
1958	43,048	1,409	27,181	113,215	3.157	3.294
1959	43,329	4,588	25,044	67,501	1.931	2.241
1960	44,734	6,517	24,435	123,921	2.894	3.462
1961	44,133	4,959	26,492	275,158	6.144	6.947
1962	49,094	8,364	26,849	167,028	3.374	4.119
1963	45,937	2,476	27,170	115,716	2.951	3.164
Average:						
1940–44	$20,660	$ 108	$18,682	$ 76,004	4.559	4.588
1960–63	45,975	5,579	26,237	170,456	3.815	4.400

individual portfolios within the group. When extreme stockholdings—defined, as before, to be those of a magnitude greater than two standard deviations distant from the original means for each of the five executive positions each year—are removed from consideration, the revised January 1 mean market values compiled in Table 44 emerge.[4] The per capita equity investments defined therein come to about only 20 per cent of the initial values specified in Table 37 in the early years shown, and drop to as little as 5 per cent of those values after 1960. This finding, and the similarly recalculated dividend and capital gains averages in Appendix F, unquestionably cast a somewhat different light on the executive ownership role.

The degree of difference is highlighted by the relationships recorded in Tables 45 and 46, where the modified after-tax dividend and absolute capital gains figures are compared with the new fixed-dollar and stock-based compensation means which result from eliminating extreme values of the latter as well.[5] The data indicate that income from ownership items was some four and one-half times as important as non-stock-related inflows from employment for the top men in the fifteen companies during the early 1940's, but had diminished to only 80 per cent as important by the 1960's. For the top-five executive category, the decline was from 175 per cent of fixed-dollar pay to just about matching yearly amounts over the same interval. A noticeable secular reduction in the intensity of the management-shareholder income link is therefore apparent, although annual increments to wealth roughly equal to those enjoyed from salary, bonus, pension benefits, and other fixed-sum rewards combined, still suggest a respectable level of ownership involvement. By that standard, the evidence for the small-manufacturing sample does follow—in its general character, at least—the patterns previously displayed by the two large-company groups.

[4] The new data matrix contains 1,655 observations, down 7 per cent from the original 1,781.

[5] The revised compensation averages are also contained in Appendix F. A 5 per cent reduction in sample size is embodied in those figures.

TABLE 44

Average Market Value of Executive Stockholdings: Small
Manufacturing Sample, 1940–63; Extreme Values Deleted
(amounts in dollars)

Year	Top Executive	Top Five Executives
1940	557,178	157,923
1941	583,843	146,918
1942	202,964	85,461
1943	357,364	98,302
1944	475,013	151,093
1945	471,531	157,127
1946	638,171	189,089
1947	484,145	135,465
1948	294,079	88,535
1949	142,643	52,674
1950	173,579	55,573
1951	184,953	73,619
1952	185,306	78,063
1953	168,740	58,325
1954	166,305	59,207
1955	228,245	80,778
1956	389,994	112,622
1957	395,988	121,762
1958	352,601	103,923
1959	199,571	105,223
1960	183,608	156,429
1961	186,085	108,825
1962	121,695	235,541
1963	150,368	220,335

TABLE 45

Compensation and Ownership Income:
Small Manufacturing Sample, 1940–63;
Average for the Top Executive in Each Firm,
Extreme Values Deleted

Year	Compensation		Ownership Income		Comparison	
	(1) After-Tax Fixed-Dollar Remuneration	(2) After-Tax Stock-Based Remuneration	(3) After-Tax Dividend Income	(4) Absolute After-Tax Capital Gains	(5) [(3)+(4)] / [(1)+(2)]	(6) [(2)+(3)+(4)] / (1)
1940	$33,290	$ —	$38,321	$ 75,093	3.406	3.406
1941	32,168	1,033	30,355	163,309	5.833	6.052
1942	27,249	788	7,000	61,181	2.431	2.531
1943	23,935	601	10,942	134,600	5.931	6.105
1944	25,588	—	11,941	118,279	5.089	5.089
1945	25,746	—	8,401	113,155	4.721	4.721
1946	30,877	—	10,262	88,336	3.193	3.193
1947	33,287	—	11,274	122,474	4.018	4.018
1948	41,788	—	12,159	46,404	1.401	1.401
1949	49,589	—	8,264	23,119	0.632	0.632
1950	46,927	—	11,607	35,478	1.003	1.003
1951	44,195	—	9,702	12,779	0.508	0.508
1952	44,433	39	8,411	20,136	0.641	0.643
1953	49,772	12	4,779	19,286	0.483	0.483
1954	53,998	175	4,443	49,784	1.000	1.007
1955	55,282	3,506	4,658	40,031	0.760	0.871
1956	72,024	4,040	11,394	61,620	0.959	1.069
1957	55,726	4,391	9,183	68,291	1.288	1.469
1958	55,668	4,485	12,864	149,382	2.697	2.995
1959	59,800	7,089	4,339	37,633	0.627	0.820
1960	59,258	10,907	3,627	21,381	0.356	0.606
1961	58,287	4,649	3,540	63,125	1.059	1.223
1962	56,068	21,418	2,546	21,370	0.308	0.808
1963	60,010	1,110	3,444	41,706	0.738	0.770
Average:						
1940–44	$28,446	$ 484	$19,712	$110,492	4.501	4.594
1960–63	58,406	9,521	3,289	36,896	0.592	0.851

TABLE 46

Compensation and Ownership Income:
Small Manufacturing Sample, 1940–63;
Averages for the Top Five Executives in Each Firm,
Extreme Values Deleted

Year	Compensation		Ownership Income		Comparison	
	(1) After-Tax Fixed-Dollar Remuneration	(2) After-Tax Stock-Based Remuneration	(3) After-Tax Dividend Income	(4) Absolute After-Tax Capital Gains	(5) $\frac{[(3)+(4)]}{[(1)+(2)]}$	(6) $\frac{[(2)+(3)+(4)]}{(1)}$
1940	$23,299	$ –	$9,820	$19,190	1.245	1.245
1941	21,620	235	7,514	40,327	2.188	2.223
1942	19,653	182	3,439	18,850	1.123	1.143
1943	17,290	143	3,384	33,109	2.093	2.118
1944	17,749	–	3,828	34,512	2.160	2.160
1945	19,163	–	3,234	36,312	2.063	2.063
1946	22,092	–	3,411	27,693	1.407	1.407
1947	25,449	–	3,482	27,065	1.200	1.200
1948	30,714	–	3,835	14,039	0.581	0.581
1949	32,245	–	2,893	7,348	0.317	0.317
1950	32,279	–	3,431	10,073	0.418	0.418
1951	32,674	–	3,712	6,774	0.320	0.320
1952	32,301	69	3,062	5,789	0.273	0.276
1953	36,956	193	2,037	6,359	0.226	0.232
1954	36,929	52	2,080	17,134	0.519	0.521
1955	38,055	1,610	2,214	15,543	0.447	0.508
1956	42,481	2,186	3,526	23,402	0.602	0.685
1957	39,929	1,499	3,112	20,587	0.572	0.631
1958	40,218	1,276	3,867	43,656	1.145	1.213
1959	42,552	4,668	2,806	16,346	0.405	0.559
1960	44,734	6,517	3,877	23,630	0.536	0.760
1961	43,809	4,585	2,830	35,600	0.794	0.981
1962	44,934	8,232	5,500	37,257	0.804	1.134
1963	44,572	1,232	5,449	46,409	1.132	1.191
Average:						
1940–44	$19,922	$ 112	$5,597	$29,197	1.737	1.752
1960–63	44,512	5,142	4,414	35,724	0.808	1.017

Proportionate Holdings

One substantial departure from those patterns can, however, be discerned. The top officers of the smaller corporations have consistently owned much larger *fractions* of their firms' outstanding common shares than was the case for either of the other two samples. Table 47 summarizes the findings, and may be contrasted with the large-industrial and retail-trade data in Tables 25 and 36. According to the full-sample averages, in 1940 the highest-paid individuals in the fifteen small manufacturing companies held in their portfolios more than 12 per cent of their firm's equity securities. The five highest-paid executives together held nearly 15 per cent. Both of these figures conjure up visions of the kind of classic entrepreneur-administrator which the usual discussion of the small-firm operation implies. While the two ownership proportions at issue fell to 4.7 and 6.9 per cent, respectively, by 1963, they continued to denote significant minority interests. The reduced-sample means scale down that interpretation to some extent, but do portray holdings which are anywhere from three to sixteen times greater in comparison with company size than are those observed among larger enterprises.

Market Activity

To complete the parallel, we may inquire as to the volume of trading in their own firm's securities which the relevant senior executives have undertaken. As it turns out, a transaction of any sort which altered the number of common shares held occurred during just 523 of the 1,781 man-years of compensation and ownership experience that comprise the full-sample data matrix (i.e., within only 29 per cent of the set of possible intervals). Fully 348 of the changes, moreover, involved *increases* in holdings, leaving a mere 175 transactions —less than one in every 10 man-years investigated—which resulted in a net sale of shares by top management. Both rates are well below the retail trade and large manufacturing portfolio turnover figures, evincing not only a heavier relative commitment to employer-com-

TABLE 47

Trends in Proportionate Ownership:
Small Manufacturing Sample, 1940–63

	1940	1963
Full Sample		
Mean per capita stockholdings:		
Top executives	$2,732,158	$3,489,437
Top five executives	$637,434	$1,033,769
Implied total holdings:		
15 top executives	$40,982,370	$52,341,555
75 top five executives	$47,807,550	$77,532,675
Total market value of the 15 sample corporations	$325,089,000	$1,123,627,000
Fraction of total owned by executives:		
Top executives	12.607%	4.658%
Top five executives	14.706%	6.900%
Reduced Sample with Extreme Values Deleted		
Mean per capita stockholdings:		
Top executives	$557,178	$150,368
Top five executives	$157,923	$220,335
Implied total holdings:		
15 top executives	$8,357,670	$2,255,520
75 top five executives	$11,844,225	$16,525,125
Total market value of the 15 sample corporations	$325,089,000	$1,123,627,000
Fraction of total owned by executives:		
Top executives	2.571%	0.201%
Top five executives	3.643%	1.471%

pany stock by the present sample but a more permanent individual attachment to those investments.

Summary

The top administrative officers of a representative group of small to medium-size American manufacturing corporations have maintained equity holdings in their respective firms ranging between $1 million and $4 million per capita during the early 1960's, up from figures approximately half as great prior to World War II. The dividends and capital gains associated with these holdings have amounted to as much as $1 million per executive within a given calendar year, and have averaged some $200,000 to $500,000 annually from 1960 through 1963. At such levels, the indicated returns far surpassed, in the aggregate, the concurrent cash receipts and deferred income values which executives commanded as remuneration in their capacity as employees. The removal from the data of extraordinary stockholding and compensation experiences has a marked impact on the historical record, but it does no more than reduce mean ownership income flows to about the volume of mean total managerial earnings. Even given this adjustment, therefore, a strong interdependence of executive and shareholder economic well-being appears to prevail.

7

SUMMARY AND EVALUATION

THE ISSUE OF THE RELATIONSHIP between the personal economic objectives of the senior corporate executive and the pecuniary interests of his firm's common stockholders has been a topic for scholarly discussion ever since it became apparent that the large aggregations of scarce resources demanded by industrialization would require an increasingly professionalized managerial group for successful administration. The consequent separation of the capital-supply and capital-management functions raised the possibility that the decision-making process within the firm would take on a different character, and be directed toward different goals, than was true in a simpler commercial environment wherein the two functions resided in the same individuals. The usual conclusion in the literature of business and economics over the past several decades has been that this possibility has indeed become a reality, and that a viable mechanism no longer exists for eliciting a congruence of managerial and ownership objectives in the operation of the widely held corporate enterprise.

The task of the present investigation has been to raise anew the question of the soundness of that conclusion. Because our tax laws encourage corporations to reward their employees through devices which depend for their value on the market price behavior of the company's common shares, and because even a casual inspection of annual proxy statements suggests that many top executives maintain significant direct equity investments in their own firms, the chance that a more important link than was generally recognized existed between the personal income of management and the returns which shareholders enjoy seemed worth examining. The evidence offered in the preceding chapters appears to support this hypothesis. The annual income of executives depends very heavily, very directly, and very persistently, on the dividends received and capital gains experienced by such men in their roles both as stockholders of their employer companies, and as beneficiaries of stock-related compensation arrangements. Accordingly, the often-expressed concern that the professional manager is likely to display a massive indifference to the traditional profit-seeking orientation of the firm is regarded here with skepticism, despite the unarguable shift from entrepreneurship to administration as the dominant activity of the executive class.

The Data

The senior officers of three categories of firms were chosen as the sample to which the analysis was addressed. The main focus was on a group of fifty large manufacturing corporations, with data from fifteen small manufacturers and fifteen chain-store retailing organizations being compiled to supplement and test the broader applicability of the initial findings. The investigation covered the period from 1940 through 1963, thereby encompassing an interval in which a number of major structural changes occurred in the economy. Out of the extensive body of evidence developed, the particular set of figures which seems to provide the best summary of the historical record is gathered in Table 48 and depicted in Chart 17. These figures portray the ratio, year by year, of total ownership-related after-tax personal executive income to concurrent after-tax fixed-dollar employee remuneration for all three company samples. The group considered consists of the five highest-paid individuals in each firm taken together, and the underlying data are the mean annual values determined after exclusion of extreme observations of stock-holding and compensation. Thus, the time series shown are the final columns of Tables 24, 35, and 46, above, in which the relationships between ownership income and remuneration were documented for the top-five category in the three samples separately.

These figures are taken to represent the most suitable synthesis of the results of the analysis because, first of all, they do abstract from the effects of extraordinary individual circumstances. While the full-sample averages would tell a much more impressive story, they are apt to be misleading as measures of the norm for the relevant

TABLE 48

The Importance of Ownership Income to Senior Executives:
A Summary for the Years 1940 Through 1963 for the Top Five
Executives in Each Firm, Extreme Values Deleted

Ratio of Dividends Plus Absolute Capital Gains Plus Stock
Compensation to Fixed-Dollar Earnings

Year	Large Manufacturers	Retail Trade	Small Manufacturers
1940	0.757	0.443	1.245
1941	0.684	0.766	2.223
1942	0.830	0.501	1.143
1943	1.039	1.482	2.118
1944	0.741	0.951	2.160
1945	1.466	3.168	2.063
1946	0.685	1.069	1.407
1947	0.441	0.568	1.200
1948	0.230	0.357	0.581
1949	0.434	0.504	0.317
1950	0.690	0.863	0.418
1951	0.595	0.389	0.320
1952	0.636	0.304	0.276
1953	0.524	0.262	0.232
1954	1.887	0.784	0.521
1955	1.502	0.635	0.508
1956	1.520	0.440	0.685
1957	1.627	0.326	0.631
1958	3.007	1.047	1.213
1959	2.170	0.654	0.559
1960	2.803	0.832	0.760
1961	3.425	1.675	0.981
1962	2.673	0.899	1.134
1963	2.287	1.307	1.191
Averages for:			
1940–44	0.799	0.801	1.752
1960–63	2.795	1.178	1.017

CHART 17

RATIO OF OWNERSHIP INCOME ITEMS TO FIXED-DOLLAR
EXECUTIVE EARNINGS, 1940-63

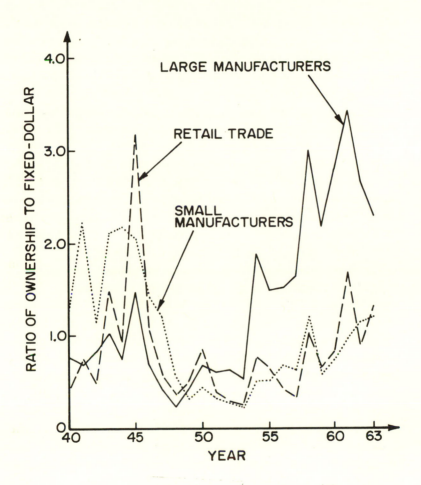

managerial group. The severe impact of eliminating extreme values from the small-manufacturing data perhaps best illustrates this concern. Secondly, it seems desirable to cast up the findings from as broad a base as possible. Even though the differences between the experience of the highest-paid man in each firm, and the five highest-paid together, turned out to be of interest in several contexts, the latter group—which is the largest the available proxy statement information permits to be examined—serves as the better vehicle for summarizing over-all income patterns at the senior executive level. Finally, the addition of the value of stock-related compensation to annual dividends and capital gains in making comparisons with fixed-dollar earnings provides a more comprehensive index of the true degree of executive exposure to the contingencies and uncertainties of ownership than the dividends and gains alone would furnish. The securities market's response to the firm's activities is as much a determinant of the worth of stock-based pay arrangements as it is the genesis of shareholder returns. For these reasons, Table 48 and Chart 17 appear to combine the most meaningful, as well as the most comprehensive, elements of the historical income profile.

The impression they convey is one of substantial involvement on the part of executives in the ongoing rewards and penalties of an equity or equitylike position. The average annual after-tax increments to personal managerial wealth which arose from ownership-connected income sources after 1960 exceeded the corresponding increments from fixed-dollar employee remuneration for all three samples. In the case of large manufacturing company executives, in particular, ownership items were nearly three times the size of fixed-dollar earnings. The conclusion therefore would be that the personal economic well-being of the senior professional manager is, of necessity, tied very closely to that of his firm's shareholders—sufficiently closely, in the view here, as to imply that the pursuit of administrative policies inimical to the profit objectives of shareholders would be irrational in terms of the man's own self-interest. A finding that the executive stands to gain much more from the successful operation of the firm than from the mere retention of his job follows, it should be emphasized, from an investigation which has focused on precisely those large and widely held enterprises that are most frequently cited as examples of the disengagement of management from ownership attitudes and sanctions. As it happens, executives are not insulated from the consequences of poor company performance—even in the short run—and are demonstrably able to reap significant benefits from a successful situation.

The pattern of changes over the years in the strength of the owner-ship income link is also worth noting. For both the large-manufactur-ing, and retail-trade, samples, ownership returns were *more* important in the 1960's than they had been during the early 1940's, whereas a decline is observable for the senior officers of small-manufacturing firms. A consistent tendency toward a growing importance in all three cases would, of course, reinforce the interpretation placed here on the data. A more careful look at the findings, however—especially as portrayed in Chart 17—suggests that a generalized upward trend is indeed present. The ratio of dividends plus gains plus stock com-pensation to fixed-dollar inflows can be seen to have bottomed out in the late 1940's and early 1950's for every sample, and to have risen in a clear and fairly steady manner ever since.[1] The fact that the ratios in the 1960's for the small-manufacturing sample are still below their prewar levels thus seems less relevant than the evidence as to what has been happening in the interim. From that standpoint, an increasing secular role in the executive income structure for own-ership elements is apparent throughout. This phenomenon can be expected to continue in the future if only as a consequence of the growing reliance by corporations on stock-related pay arrangements for their top officials. The analysis in Chapter 3 of the managerial compensation package enjoyed by all three groups amply documents this expectation.

One feature of the data in recent years which runs particularly counter to the usual folklore is the greater relative dependence of income on stock price changes and company dividends evinced among executives of very large firms as compared with their counterparts in smaller organizations. Quite the reverse circumstance would almost

[1] The availability to executives of such instruments as stock options, begin-ning in the early 1950's, undoubtedly contributed to this recovery of ownership.

certainly be the prediction in most of the current literature.[2] As we found earlier, differences both in the magnitude of the stockholdings in question and in the use of stock-based instruments of remuneration account for this conclusion. Whatever their source, the figures belie the contention that the more a growing enterprise requires professional administration, the less likely are the interests of shareholders to be translated into an effective personal monetary payoff for management consistent with those interests.[3]

Commentary

The foregoing arguments, it may be recalled, would be buttressed substantially were we to employ the full-sample time series of Tables 19, 32, and 43 in the comparisons. Moreover, the figures in Table 48 almost certainly understate the case as they stand, because it has been assumed implicitly in our discussions that there is no real connection between any of the *fixed-dollar* rewards which executives receive and the performance of their companies. To the extent that such a relationship does exist, the income link reported here will emerge in still bolder relief. That issue has been addressed elsewhere by the author with encouraging results.[4] There turns out to be a definite and persistent correlation between the salaries and bonuses of the senior corporate executives in the large-manufacturing sample [5] and the profits and equity market values of their employer firms. By

---

[2] And quite the reverse can, of course, be seen in Table 48 to have been true during the 1940's.

[3] There is, on the other hand, the possibility of some bias in this respect in the small-firm sample. Since the information contained in corporate proxy statements is necessary to the analysis—and since closely held firms where the management and ownership groups are one and the same are not ordinarily forced by SEC regulations to issue proxy statements—we may end up including in the sample predominantly those smaller firms in which management's equity position *is* fairly small. Nonetheless, the point that large company size is by no means a deterrent to a significant interdependence between executive incomes and stockholder returns is strongly supported by the data.

[4] W. G. Lewellen and A. B. Huntsman, "Managerial Pay and Corporate Performance," *American Economic Review*, Vol. LX, No. 4 (September 1970).

[5] Only the large-manfacturing sample was examined in this manner, since the sample sizes in the retail trade and small-manufacturing groups were too small to allow the execution of meaningful statistical tests of significance.

the same token, it was found that no systematic link between cash compensation and the most commonly proposed nonprofit measure of company size—annual sales volume—could be established. Thus, in a cross-sectional multiple regression framework, the profit and equity market value coefficients tested as significant at the .01 level in virtually every year, whereas the sales coefficients were nowhere significant. Those elements of the managerial pay package which are not *automatically* tied to company success as shareholders perceive it, can therefore be shown to be tied indirectly through extant corporate compensation practices.

The Compensation Record

While the historical evidence relating to executive remuneration has been utilized primarily as a frame of reference for a treatment of the impact of stock ownership patterns, that evidence merits some attention in its own right. We observe that total after-tax executive pay—whether defined for the highest-paid indivduals in the respective firms or for the five highest-paid combined—almost exactly doubled between 1940 and 1963 within each sample at issue. The consistency of this finding for three such diverse segments of the economy is striking enough to imply that the phenomenon may be a general characteristic of the structure of managerial rewards, as it has developed during the last quarter-century under the pressure of major revisions in federal tax policy. The impact of taxes is clearly discernible, both in the shift away from direct cash payments over time toward an increasing emphasis on deferred and contingent compensation devices for all firms, and in the interfirm differences within given years in the implementation of those devices. For example, large manufacturing corporations—wherein the aggregate levels of executive remuneration were highest—relied most heavily on noncurrent rewards as vehicles for sidestepping the effect of progressive ordinary personal tax rates. The somewhat smaller amounts of compensation recorded among the retail trade group were comprised proportionately less of deferred arrangements, and the still lower-paying small manufacturing sample emphasized cash compensation most strongly. The logic of tax planning, therefore, appears to have made the appropriate impression. Recognition that many of the newer deferred and contingent instruments adopted are designed around shares of the employer corporation's common stock as the means of payment is, of course, a key element in our investigation of the management-shareholder income relationship.

Ownership Proportions

A sidelight to that relationship is the secular decline in the fraction of their firm's outstanding equity securities which senior executives hold. A drop from 1940 to 1963 in percentage ownership occurred in each of the three samples, although the usefulness of this observation must be qualified by noting that the holdings involved were so small throughout—i.e., most often in the range of 1 per cent or less of the outstanding shares of the sample companies—that even large variations within that range do not appear to be of much real significance. A decline of this sort is, nonetheless, a standard bench mark for discussions which seek to establish the progressive dissociation of management from an identification with shareholder interests. While not denying that today's executives do own a rather smaller fraction of their companies' total common stock than was true of their predecessors in 1940, the contention here is that the relative importance of the income flows attendant upon such ownership in the aggregate *personal* income profile of the individual executive should be our concern instead. So long as those flows account for as much of observable annual increments to wealth as they currently do, a sensitivity by management to the shareholder viewpoint seems a reasonable expectation, regardless of whether or not substantial percentage minority ownership positions are involved.

Portfolio Turnover

Another dimension of the executive's stance toward the organization for which he works has to do with the degree to which the portfolio commitments in the company's shares that he undertakes are speculative in nature. If we should discover that the senior management group is continually engaged in a great deal of short-term trading, riding the peaks and troughs of market sentiment on inside information, this would negate the conclusion that an effective and beneficial exposure to the ongoing contingencies of ownership prevails. Quite the reverse situation, however, is indicated by the data. Executives overwhelmingly buy and hold, as evidenced by the finding that in the large-manufacturing and retail-trade samples, transactions which resulted in a reduction in a man's own-firm stockholdings occurred, on the average, in just one out of every six years of his career experience. In the case of the small-manufacturing category, the rate was an even lower one year out of ten. Put differently, the annual capital gains and losses listed in the comparisons with executive compensation are predominantly *accrued* rather than *realized* increments, implying that the typical upper-level professional manager in fact foregoes possible speculative profits in favor of the kind of long-term participation in company fortunes that would support the arguments offered here.

The Remainder of the Portfolio

One aspect of the personal circumstances of the men in the sample which has not been examined, and which would bear on the credibility of the conclusions drawn, concerns the role which the observed employer-company stockholdings play in the *total* executive securities portfolio. We may be able to assert that the dividends, capital gains, and stock-related rewards which result from an individual's employment and investment association with his firm dominate the total income flows generated from *that* source, but the inference that this is an important phenomenon in terms of identifying with shareholder objectives would lose some of its impact if the men involved had such large *aggregate* securities portfolios that the items we can measure were trivial in comparison with the dividends, capital gains, and interest earnings from other investments. Since no data exist which permit a determination of the size of the remainder of executive portfolios—holdings only in one's own company being reported in proxy statements—it is difficult to assess the extent to which the analysis would be modified by a more comprehensive set of figures.

There is cause to suspect that the bulk of senior management's investments must indeed be comprised of employer-company shares if only because the magnitude of the holdings we *can* observe already surpasses what would seem a reasonable expectation of total executive wealth. A finding that average per capita ownership positions are in the neighborhood of $2.5 million (for the full-sample large manufacturing group) or even $1 million (when extreme values are eliminated) exceeds by a substantial margin at least this writer's *ex ante* notions of likely dollar amounts. Offhand, it is hard to see how these men could have funds left for alternative portfolio commitments.

Furthermore, if we believe that executives, like other investors, are most comfortable when investing with knowledge, we would expect them to be strongly attracted to their own corporation's securities simply because they know more about those firms than they do about any others. Considerations of broad portfolio diversification might, in short, be given less *personal* weight by top management than by the investment community in general. These interpretations are, however, quite unsupported by empirical evidence and must remain conjectural. Clearly, there is a need for additional research. The feeling here is that just as ownership returns predominate in the observable executive income profile, so do employer-company stockholdings predominate in the total executive securities portfolio. Nonetheless, it must be admitted that if the latter contention should prove incorrect, the implications of the former would be diluted.

The Merger Trend

On the other side of the coin, there have been some recent developments in the business environment which should operate to heighten senior executives' sensitivity to the issue of profit maximization or share price maximization, even apart from the factors considered in the current discussion. Beginning in the 1960's, a significant upsurge in the frequency—some might say, the audacity—of corporate merger efforts has become apparent, resulting in the formation of a wide variety of so-called conglomerate enterprises. The intensity of this activity suggests that very few top management groups nowadays can afford the luxury of less than full attention toward utilizing their company's resources in an efficient manner, on penalty of having some more vigorous organization go over their heads directly to shareholders with the promise of improved performance. Today's captains of industry, in effect, expose themselves to the distinct prospect of being demoted to lieutenants if they do not address their responsibilities in a way that produces adequate returns to owners. The fact that the demotion is apt to originate with some third party makes it no less a real concern, and the demonstrated skill of that third party in implementing the rebellion may make the threat more persuasive than one arising from a coalition of dissatisfied current stockholders.

Summary

The contention, then, is that there exist a number of mechanisms which should go a long way toward overcoming any tendency for the separation of corporate owners and managers in the contemporary economy to be accompanied by a separation of their respective interests and objectives. The attempt has been to document—and to appraise the dimensions of—what seems likely to be the most important such mechanism: the link between executives' personal incomes and the market returns to shareholders. Upon investigation of the historical compensation and ownership experience of a large and diverse sample of senior corporate officers, that link has been shown to be strong, immediate, and persistent. While the evidence presented obviously cannot be described as a *proof* that executives will necessarily perform their duties with the welfare of stockholders paramount in their minds, it can be offered as clear support for the proposition that it would be very much in their self-interest to do so. The findings are at least consistent with the notion that "what's good for the company is good for the executive." To date, the contrary viewpoint has not had the benefit of similar hard evidence.

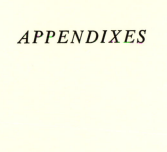

APPENDIXES

APPENDIX A: NUMERICAL EXAMPLE
OF COMPENSATION CALCULATIONS

To illustrate the analytical approach used in measuring the worth of the elements in the managerial pay package by means of "current income equivalents," the "typical" case history shown in Table A-1 was derived by averaging the year-to-year compensation experience of the some 550 different individual executives who comprised the large manufacturing sample. The tabulation records the mean values, by age, of the salaries, bonuses, pension benefit expectations, and other elements of remuneration enjoyed by those executives during the years in which they appeared in the sample. As such, it represents, of course, a composite set of circumstances rather than the history of any observable single individual.

We find that the typical manufacturing executive spent a total of 14 years in the sample. He was forty-nine years old by the time he attained a position in his firm sufficiently important to make his earnings of interest here.[1] During that first year, he received $61,750 before taxes in the form of direct cash salary and bonus payments, was promised $4,040 in annual noncontributory pension benefits upon retirement, and was required to contribute $510 toward the financing of a prospective annual contributory pension amounting to $3,600. He was, in addition, the beneficiary of a deferred compensation arrangement under which he was to receive $130 each year beginning at age sixty-five and continuing for nine years. The remainder of the table lists the corresponding magnitudes for each subsequent year of the man's employment.[2] We see that his current cash

---

[1] The nature of this threshold is discussed in Chapter 2.

[2] The fact that he turns out to leave the sample after age sixty-two can be explained in part by the effects of early retirement, death, and job mobility on the averages. The most influential factor, however, is purely technical: because

A Representative Compensation Experience
(amounts in dollars)

Executive Age	Salary Plus Bonus Receipts	Expected Annual Noncontributory Pension Benefit	Expected Annual Contributory Pension Benefit	Executive's Annual Contributions to His Pension	Expected Annual Deferred Compensation Payment [a]
49	61,750	4,040	3,600	510	130
50	65,290	4,940	4,340	610	170
51	68,210	5,490	4,990	700	210
52	72,790	5,930	5,270	760	310
53	74,660	6,790	5,730	860	500
54	76,710	6,980	6,200	910	690
55	83,130	7,430	6,740	980	730
56	84,880	7,830	7,260	1,100	1,140
57	91,000	8,740	8,220	1,270	1,710
58	97,950	9,520	9,250	1,460	2,290
59	107,620	11,070	10,350	1,610	2,670
60	114,630	11,830	11,370	1,770	3,360
61	121,560	11,810	12,330	1,910	4,600
62	132,180	12,960	12,870	1,940	5,890

[a] Payable for nine years, beginning at retirement.

earnings somewhat better than double over the interval shown, the pension he is promised approximately triples, and his deferred pay prospects increase by a factor of better than 45 times. While, on the average, the men in the sample also received two stock option grants apiece to supplement the rewards tabulated, the options are omitted here in order to limit the range of calculations required and to keep the dimensions of the presentation manageable. Since our concern, at the moment, is with the general character of the analytical results

the data collected end with the year 1963, there are in the group a number of executives whose histories are terminated in mid-career and who, therefore, are below the normal retirement age of sixty-five when their experience ceases to be of interest.

rather than with the details of the computations, this seems a defensible decision.[3] In the same vein, the federal personal income tax schedule which was in effect during the period 1954 to 1963 will be used throughout in determining the relevant tax liabilities so as to render the year-to-year comparisons consistent.

The outcome of applying to these data the valuation framework summarized in Chapter 2 is as indicated in Table A-2. Thus, when his outside income and the deductions and exemptions he was likely to claim are taken into consideration, the executive whose experience is depicted is estimated to have enjoyed, at age forty-nine, a post-tax cash income from salary and bonus receipts amounting to $38,560. In that year, it would have been necessary for him to pay a total of $3,550 in premiums to an insurance company in order to begin the purchase of an individual retirement annuity having an after-tax present value, from his standpoint, equal to the combined after-tax present value of his anticipated contributory and noncontributory pension benefits, net of the present value of the contributions he could expect to make between ages forty-nine and sixty-four at a rate of $510 per year. The $3,550 represents the *annual* premium that would have been required if such payments were scheduled to be made by the executive to the insurer[4] from ages forty-nine through sixty-four. The employer corporation involved would, in consequence, have had to raise his annual after-tax cash income by that amount if it had chosen to reward him as well via direct payments as by the two pension promises. In the terminology here, therefore, $3,550 is denoted the "after-tax current income equivalent" of the man's pension prospects as of age forty-nine.[5]

---

[3] An illustration of the procedures involved for stock options can be found in Lewellen, *op. cit.,* pp. 56–58 and pp. 271–275.

[4] The premium rates built into these calculations in the study were obtained by averaging the figures quoted for nonparticipating individual retirement annuities by two large insurance companies—Connecticut General and Travelers, both of Hartford, Connecticut—for the calendar year in question in each instance. The nonparticipating feature meant that estimates of subsequent policy dividends were not necessary in the computations.

[5] It should be pointed out that an annual premium of this size does not necessarily permit the purchase of an individual annuity which provides for a payment in retirement to the executive which matches the aggregate $7,640 yearly benefit anticipated by him under the two pension arrangements shown. Since

TABLE A-2

Analysis of a Representative Compensation Experience
(amounts in dollars)

Executive Age	After-Tax Salary Plus Bonus Earnings	Pension After-Tax Current Income Equivalent	Deferred Compensation After-Tax Current Income Equivalent	Total After-Tax Compensation
49	38,560	3,550	30	42,140
50	40,240	4,350	40	44,630
51	41,550	4,970	50	46,570
52	43,600	5,360	80	49,040
53	44,440	6,180	150	50,770
54	45,350	6,620	230	52,200
55	48,040	7,340	240	55,620
56	48,770	8,080	450	57,300
57	51,270	9,810	780	61,860
58	53,970	11,700	1,150	66,820
59	57,590	15,050	1,430	74,070
60	60,130	17,640	2,070	79,840
61	62,640	19,110	3,550	85,300
62	66,250	23,150	5,580	94,980

Upon extending this analysis, the corresponding current income equivalent of the indicated deferred compensation arrangement turns out to be $30. That figure defines the additional annual after-tax payment to him which, if supplied by his firm beginning immediately and continuing *up to* his retirement, would have the same present value as the after-tax receipts he expects to enjoy from the deferred

both the tax treatment and benefit structures of individual annuities and corporate pension plans differ somewhat, and since an executive often must make contributions to the corporation's plan, it is typically not the case that a $10,000 individual annuity will have the same prospective after-tax present value as a $10,000 pension promise. A full discussion of these phenomena is contained in Lewellen, *op. cit.*, pp. 16–34. The pertinent differences are, in any case, reflected appropriately in the current income equivalent figures generated here and throughout the study.

payments promised *in* retirement. As was true in connection with his pension benefits, the possibility that the executive involved—here forty-nine years old—may not, in fact, live long enough to claim the full amount of either the deferred pay or its contrived annual current income equivalent is recognized explicitly in the attendant present value calculations by incorporating therein a discount for mortality as well as for time deferral.[6] Having made those calculations, we may combine the several results with the salary and bonus figures and assert that the aggregate value of the man's compensation package during the initial year tabulated was $42,140 after taxes. Had he been paid entirely in cash, take-home earnings of that magnitude would have duplicated the income, both direct and indirect, he experienced from all of his various actual rewards.

In the following year, his pre-tax salary-plus-bonus receipts increased to $65,290, giving rise to a gain of $1,680 to a total of $40,240 after taxes (estimates of deductions, exemptions, and outside income again being considered). Because his combined pension benefit expectation similarly grew by more than enough to offset in value the higher personal yearly contributions of $610 now required of him, the pension's current income equivalent jumps to $4,350. The extra $800 over the previous year denotes the incremental annual premium—payable at this point from ages fifty through sixty-four— which would add sufficient benefits to the original individual retirement annuity to augment its present value to the same extent as the net gain in value of the relevant pensions. A revised aggregate current income equivalent is therefore created, consisting now of two overlapping "layers" of annual payments, each representing the stream of premiums that would have been needed had the executive purchased for himself a series of individual annuity benefit packages

[6] This requires, of course, that the age of each man whose compensation history is included in the sample be identified. The *Who's Who* publications cited in the text, supplemented by *Poor's Register of Corporations, Directors, and Executives* (New York, Standard and Poor's Corporation), supply the necessary data. The mortality table utilized is the 1951 Group Annuity Table for Males, which should provide a reasonable representation of the longevity characteristics of individuals covered by corporate pension plans during the time period at issue empirically. See Lewellen, *op. cit.*, pp. 24–25 and pp. 297–298.

having respective after-tax present values equal to the particular (incremental) set of pension benefit promises which were made to him in particular—and successive—years.

By the same reasoning, the current income equivalent of the man's deferred compensation is shown to rise to $40. The increase of $10 from the initial year would, if the executive could look forward to it annually in the form of an after-tax addition to his salary, be perceived by him as embodying a present value matching that provided by the observed modest jump in his deferred pay prospects. His total direct and indirect after-tax earnings for the year from the three compensation sources in question thereupon come to $44,630, a gain of $2,490 from the corresponding figure computed for him in the preceding year.[7]

It should not be necessary to trace through the remainder of our typical man's employment history with the same care, given the pattern of results we now see emerging. Each time his salary and bonus or either of his two retirement income arrangements change, a recalculation is made and an increment to the appropriate current income equivalents is determined. By the time his experience is no longer of concern, a comprehensive profile of his chronological earnings has been developed. We are able to specify how much of his earnings arise from particular devices in a way that not only permits precise statements about the man's own circumstances, but also makes possible meaningful comparisons of his total pay and its components with those of other executives. It is this kind of profile of the structure of managerial rewards toward which the original compensation study was directed, the resultant figures providing the background to the current investigation.[8]

[7] In making the calculations, the partial interdependence of the value of an executive's deferred compensation and his pension benefits is taken into account throughout. For example, if the deferred pay promise increases but the pension does not, the consequence of a progressive tax structure will be to raise the overall effective tax rate anticipated in retirement on the pension because of the larger aggregate taxable income now expected from both sources combined. The implied lower present value of the pension will show up as a reduction in its after-tax current income equivalent.

[8] As was noted earlier, the only other existing study having a broadly similar objective is that by Burgess (*op. cit.*). His methodology and that employed here differ substantially, however.

APPENDIX B: CORPORATIONS IN THE THREE SAMPLES

1. *The Large Manufacturing Sample*

Allied Chemical

American Can

American Cyanamid

American Metal Climax

American Tobacco

Anaconda

Bendix

Bethlehem Steel

Boeing

Borden

Caterpillar Tractor

Cities Service

Continental Can

Continental Oil

Douglas Aircraft

Dow Chemical

DuPont

Eastman Kodak

Firestone Tire

General Electric

General Foods

General Motors

General Tire

B. F. Goodrich

Goodyear Tire

Gulf Oil

Inland Steel

IBM

International Harvester

International Paper

IT&T

Jones & Laughlin Steel

Lockheed Aircraft

National Dairy Products

North American Aviation

Phillips Petroleum

Procter & Gamble

RCA

Republic Steel

Reynolds Tobacco

Shell Oil

Sinclair Oil

Standard Oil (Indiana)

Swift

Texaco

Tidewater Oil

United Aircraft

U.S. Rubber

U.S. Steel

Westinghouse Electric

2. *The Retail Trade Sample*

Allied Stores

Associated Dry Goods

Federated Department Stores

Gimbel Brothers

W. T. Grant

Interstate Department Stores

S. S. Kresge

R. H. Macy

Marshall Field

May Department Stores

Montgomery Ward

J. C. Penney

Sears Roebuck

Walgreen

Woolworth

3. *The Small Manufacturing Sample*

Briggs & Stratton

Collins & Aikman

Consolidated Cigar

Cooper–Bessemer

Endicott Johnson

Foster–Wheeler

Gardner–Denver

Harbison–Walker Refractories

Maytag

McCall

National Can

Sharon Steel

U.S. Pipe & Foundry

Ward Foods

Wrigley

APPENDIX C: SAMPLE SIZES, BY YEAR AND EXECUTIVE RANK

TABLE C-1

Large Manufacturing Sample

	Executive Rank by Total Compensation				
Year	First	Second	Third	Fourth	Fifth
1940	49	47	43	43	40
1941	49	47	47	43	42
1942	49	47	47	42	45
1943	49	48	47	45	43
1944	50	48	47	46	45
1945	50	49	47	44	45
1946	50	49	47	46	44
1947	50	49	49	46	44
1948	50	50	50	47	42
1949	50	50	50	47	43
1950	50	50	49	49	45
1951	50	50	49	46	46
1952	50	50	47	47	45
1953	50	49	46	47	40
1954	50	49	46	45	41
1955	50	50	46	43	37
1956	50	48	46	42	31
1957	50	47	44	40	29
1958	50	48	40	38	29
1959	49	48	38	32	29
1960	49	46	33	32	24
1961	48	44	32	27	23
1962	47	40	30	24	19
1963	46	37	30	21	13

TABLE C-2

Retail Trade Sample

	Executive Rank by Total Compensation				
Year	First	Second	Third	Fourth	Fifth
1940	15	15	14	14	13
1941	14	15	14	13	14
1942	15	14	15	15	15
1943	14	15	15	15	15
1944	14	15	15	15	15
1945	15	15	15	15	15
1946	15	15	15	15	15
1947	15	15	15	15	14
1948	15	15	15	15	14
1949	15	15	15	15	14
1950	15	15	15	14	15
1951	15	15	14	15	15
1952	15	15	15	14	15
1953	15	15	14	15	15
1954	15	15	14	15	15
1955	14	15	15	15	15
1956	15	15	15	15	15
1957	15	15	15	15	15
1958	15	15	15	15	14
1959	15	15	15	15	13
1960	15	15	15	15	13
1961	15	15	15	15	12
1962	15	15	15	15	11
1963	15	15	15	14	11

−32,338	−27,48
−27,103	−23,03
11,904	10,11
27,472	23,35
28,553	24,27
61,778	52,51
−21,573	−18,33
−4,299	−3,65
−3,621	−3,07
21,006	17,85
41,448	35,23
30,167	25,642
30,778	26,161
−7,459	−6,340
141,504	120,278
96,081	81,669
60,254	51,216
−77,961	−66,267
247,709	210,553
116,864	99,334
,864 −96,625	−82,131
,459 172,199	146,369
,232 −142,159	−120,835
,696 163,444	138,927

Year					
1944	15	15	15	15	15
1945	15	15	15	15	14
1946	15	15	15	15	15
1947	15	15	15	15	15
1948	15	15	15	15	15
1949	15	15	15	15	15
1950	15	15	15	15	15
1951	15	15	15	15	15
1952	15	15	15	15	15
1953	15	15	15	15	15
1954	15	15	15	15	15
1955	15	15	15	15	15
1956	15	15	15	15	15
1957	15	15	15	15	15
1958	15	15	15	15	14
1959	15	15	15	15	14
1960	15	15	14	14	14
1961	15	15	15	15	12
1962	15	15	15	15	13
1963	15	15	15	15	11

APPENDIX D

AND C

LARGE M

ADJUSTED

The following tables recor
ship income and compensa
discussed in Chapter 4, pursu
tions by the procedures describ

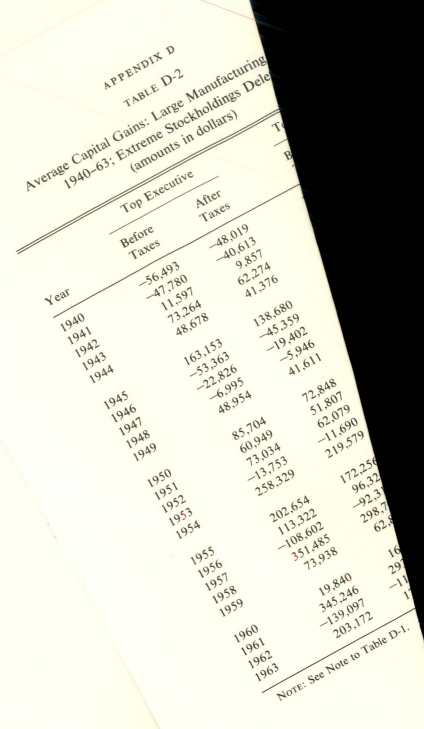

APPENDIX D

TABLE D-2

Average Capital Gains: Large Manufacturing
1940–63; Extreme Stockholdings Dele
(amounts in dollars)

| Year | Top Executive | | T |
	Before Taxes	After Taxes	B
1940	−56,493	−48,019	
1941	−47,780	−40,613	
1942	11,597	9,857	
1943	73,264	62,274	
1944	48,678	41,376	
1945	163,153	138,680	
1946	−53,363	−45,359	
1947	−22,826	−19,402	
1948	−6,995	−5,946	
1949	48,954	41,611	
1950	85,704	72,848	
1951	60,949	51,807	
1952	73,034	62,079	
1953	−13,753	−11,690	
1954	258,329	219,579	
1955	202,654	172,256	
1956	113,322	96,32	
1957	−108,602	−92,3	
1958	351,485	298,7	
1959	73,938	62,8	
1960	19,840	16	
1961	345,246	29	
1962	−139,097	−1	
1963	203,172	1	

NOTE: See Note to Table D-1.

TABLE D-3

Average Absolute Capital Gains: Large Manufacturing
Sample, 1940–63; Extreme Stockholdings Deleted
(amounts in dollars)

Year	Top Executive		Top Five Executives	
	Before Taxes	After Taxes	Before Taxes	After Taxes
1940	59,918	50,930	35,489	30,165
1941	51,634	43,888	29,572	25,136
1942	36,968	31,422	33,212	28,230
1943	76,368	64,912	40,163	34,138
1944	50,058	42,549	29,166	24,791
1945	163,153	138,680	61,778	52,511
1946	70,804	60,183	30,724	26,115
1947	48,048	40,840	18,914	16,076
1948	21,954	18,660	9,799	8,329
1949	58,180	49,453	24,707	21,000
1950	98,097	83,382	46,450	39,482
1951	84,567	71,881	38,251	32,513
1952	80,368	68,312	37,157	31,583
1953	56,255	47,816	28,585	24,297
1954	258,329	219,579	141,504	120,278
1955	220,831	187,706	102,960	87,516
1956	195,566	166,231	103,181	87,703
1957	144,435	122,769	119,667	101,716
1958	352,465	299,595	252,024	214,220
1959	143,937	122,346	160,222	136,188
1960	267,277	227,185	213,305	181,309
1961	370,300	314,755	272,525	231,646
1962	182,409	155,047	201,469	171,248
1963	218,541	185,759	174,529	148,349

NOTE: See Note to Table D-1.

TABLE D-4

Average Total After-Tax Compensation and Its Components:
Top Executives of Large Manufacturing Corporations, 1940–63;
Extreme Values Deleted
(amounts in dollars)

Year	Fixed-Dollar Rewards	Stock-Based Rewards	After-Tax Total
1940	81,524 (96)	3,435 (4)	84,959
1941	75,202 (96)	2,876 (4)	78,078
1942	58,898 (96)	2,185 (4)	61,083
1943	52,106 (96)	2,079 (4)	54,185
1944	56,226 (98)	1,369 (2)	57,595
1945	55,414 (98)	989 (2)	56,403
1946	65,348 (99)	530 (1)	65,878
1947	66,742 (99)	664 (1)	67,406
1948	91,762 (97)	2,474 (3)	94,236
1949	92,778 (95)	4,960 (5)	97,738
1950	106,414 (93)	8,378 (7)	114,792
1951	94,955 (97)	2,522 (3)	97,477
1952	92,647 (93)	7,910 (7)	100,557
1953	101,396 (89)	12,970 (11)	114,366
1954	105,101 (82)	22,990 (18)	128,091
1955	119,424 (65)	64,855 (35)	184,279
1956	124,397 (61)	80,061 (39)	204,458
1957	128,601 (61)	80,437 (39)	209,038
1958	109,804 (74)	38,769 (26)	148,573
1959	119,954 (62)	71,946 (38)	191,900
1960	115,639 (58)	82,178 (42)	197,817
1961	111,520 (60)	73,473 (40)	184,993
1962	116,356 (59)	80,575 (41)	196,931
1963	107,672 (65)	58,708 (35)	166,380
Average: 1955–63	117,041 (63)	70,111 (37)	187,152

NOTE: Figures in parentheses denote per cent of total each year.

TABLE D-5

Average Total After-Tax Compensation and Its Components:
Top Five Executives of Large Manufacturing Corporations,
1940–63; Extreme Values Deleted
(amounts in dollars)

Year	Fixed-Dollar Rewards	Stock-Based Rewards	After-Tax Total
1940	51,646 (97)	1,561 (3)	53,207
1941	47,621 (96)	1,900 (4)	49,521
1942	40,115 (97)	1,210 (3)	41,325
1943	36,404 (98)	688 (2)	37,092
1944	38,264 (98)	726 (2)	38,990
1945	38,227 (98)	612 (2)	38,839
1946	43,722 (99)	587 (1)	44,309
1947	44,464 (99)	641 (1)	45,105
1948	62,150 (98)	1,424 (2)	63,574
1949	62,792 (97)	1,685 (3)	64,477
1950	69,571 (96)	2,708 (4)	72,279
1951	68,022 (97)	2,133 (3)	70,155
1952	66,010 (93)	5,075 (7)	71,085
1953	70,285 (91)	6,964 (9)	77,249
1954	72,983 (87)	10,599 (13)	83,582
1955	81,950 (75)	27,056 (25)	109,006
1956	86,675 (71)	34,611 (29)	121,286
1957	87,355 (74)	30,747 (26)	118,102
1958	80,376 (83)	16,555 (17)	96,931
1959	83,449 (71)	33,383 (29)	116,832
1960	82,172 (69)	36,811 (31)	118,983
1961	81,272 (70)	34,371 (30)	115,643
1962	83,489 (69)	37,140 (31)	120,629
1963	82,060 (78)	23,797 (22)	105,857
Average: 1955–63	83,200 (73)	30,497 (27)	113,697

NOTE: Figures in parentheses denote per cent of total each year.

APPENDIX E: OWNERSHIP INCOME AND COMPENSATION WITHIN THE RETAIL TRADE SAMPLE: ADJUSTED FOR EXTREME VALUES

TABLE E-1

Average Dividend Receipts
(amounts in dollars)

Year	Top Executive		Top Five Executives	
	Before Taxes	After Taxes	Before Taxes	After Taxes
1940	21,091	13,750	10,353	7,032
1941	19,957	10,190	10,518	5,620
1942	25,487	11,358	9,682	4,352
1943	29,334	11,437	11,239	4,584
1944	27,637	10,912	9,844	3,909
1945	20,597	7,924	9,974	3,969
1946	31,508	12,785	12,203	5,129
1947	24,058	9,943	12,540	5,226
1948	20,671	11,857	11,277	6,387
1949	23,926	13,855	10,758	6,207
1950	43,548	24,590	13,419	7,581
1951	26,281	14,746	12,120	6,617
1952	24,888	13,277	9,777	5,209
1953	11,305	5,826	7,469	3,986
1954	8,133	4,454	9,195	5,112
1955	28,390	14,962	10,568	5,697
1956	17,776	9,506	8,877	4,822
1957	22,770	11,646	10,294	5,462
1958	-12,978	6,380	8,688	4,571
1959	15,190	7,479	9,428	4,895
1960	16,010	8,083	10,602	5,485
1961	12,236	6,039	9,963	5,277
1962	15,401	7,981	10,677	5,627
1963	17,251	8,513	12,071	6,251

TABLE E-2

Average Capital Gains: Retail Trade Sample, 1940–63; Extreme Stockholdings Deleted
(amounts in dollars)

Year	Top Executive		Top Five Executives	
	Before Taxes	After Taxes	Before Taxes	After Taxes
1940	−24,165	−20,540	−9,805	−8,334
1941	−63,755	−54,192	−30,789	−26,171
1942	22,356	19,003	9,893	8,409
1943	160,706	136,600	534,487	45,464
1944	102,060	86,751	36,045	30,638
1945	288,156	244,933	126,845	107,818
1946	−107,266	−91,176	−45,102	−38,337
1947	−48,264	−41,024	−21,019	−17,866
1948	−14,500	−12,325	−3,373	−2,867
1949	56,113	47,696	24,902	21,167
1950	142,838	121,412	42,219	35,886
1951	−26,207	−22,276	−11,725	−9,966
1952	5,534	4,704	768	653
1953	−14,779	−12,562	−8,353	−7,100
1954	41,418	35,205	45,389	38,581
1955	90,124	76,605	29,053	24,695
1956	−33,880	−28,798	−19,426	−16,512
1957	−10,291	−8,747	−3,352	−2,849
1958	98,238	83,502	68,824	58,500
1959	39,262	33,373	27,174	23,098
1960	54,885	46,652	35,375	30,069
1961	161,112	136,945	100,176	85,150
1962	−68,587	−58,299	−39,025	−33,171
1963	108,132	91,912	81,954	69,661

TABLE E-3

Average Absolute Capital Gains: Retail Trade Sample, 1940–63; Extreme Stockholdings Deleted
(amounts in dollars)

Year	Top Executive		Top Five Executives	
	Before Taxes	After Taxes	Before Taxes	After Taxes
1940	37,999	32,299	15,226	12,942
1941	64,880	55,148	31,138	26,467
1942	53,285	45,292	16,379	13,922
1943	160,706	136,600	53,487	45,464
1944	102,060	86,751	36,045	30,638
1945	288,156	244,933	126,845	107,818
1946	115,958	98,564	47,754	40,591
1947	49,288	41,895	22,998	19,548
1948	33,688	28,635	17,061	14,502
1949	61,792	52,523	26,362	22,408
1950	180,378	153,321	52,371	44,515
1951	43,491	36,967	17,655	15,007
1952	35,278	29,986	12,291	10,447
1953	18,079	15,367	10,925	9,286
1954	41,579	35,342	45,702	38,847
1955	93,869	79,789	31,825	27,051
1956	33,980	28,883	19,528	16,599
1957	30,326	25,777	11,379	9,672
1958	98,237	83,502	68,824	58,500
1959	40,324	34,275	28,476	24,205
1960	67,309	57,213	40,341	34,290
1961	161,112	136,945	100,176	85,150
1962	77,924	66,235	44,378	37,721
1963	108,556	92,273	82,222	69,889

TABLE E-4

Average Total After-Tax Compensation:
Retail Trade Sample, 1940–63;
Extreme Values Deleted
(amounts in dollars)

Year	Top Executive	Top Five Executives
1940	55,095	45,796
1941	53,512	42,482
1942	44,209	36,689
1943	41,581	34,095
1944	47,491	36,688
1945	44,404	35,969
1946	58,816	43,526
1947	56,484	44,048
1948	76,506	60,630
1949	74,248	57,710
1950	75,662	61,580
1951	69,021	57,536
1952	65,895	54,855
1953	67,389	55,717
1954	74,891	61,370
1955	84,596	67,582
1956	98,324	71,740
1957	92,550	74,803
1958	108,426	75,365
1959	115,072	82,792
1960	107,858	80,733
1961	125,530	84,601
1962	115,567	85,461
1963	112,918	83,000

APPENDIX F: OWNERSHIP INCOME AND COMPENSATION WITHIN THE SMALL MANUFACTURING SAMPLE: ADJUSTED FOR EXTREME VALUES

TABLE F-1

Average Dividend Receipts
(amounts in dollars)

Year	Top Executive		Top Five Executives	
	Before Taxes	After Taxes	Before Taxes	After Taxes
1940	50,592	38,321	12,684	9,820
1941	49,528	30,355	12,012	7,514
1942	13,878	7,000	6,143	3,439
1943	22,961	10,942	6,704	3,384
1944	25,012	11,941	7,644	3,828
1945	17,100	8,401	6,336	3,234
1946	19,435	10,262	6,365	3,411
1947	22,159	11,274	6,615	3,482
1948	19,214	12,159	5,783	3,835
1949	12,888	8,264	4,296	2,893
1950	19,251	11,607	5,385	3,431
1951	16,388	9,702	6,152	3,712
1952	15,326	8,411	5,388	3,062
1953	8,810	4,779	3,495	2,037
1954	7,675	4,443	3,373	2,080
1955	8,121	4,658	3,624	2,214
1956	20,288	11,394	5,929	3,526
1957	15,935	9,183	5,084	3,112
1958	22,803	12,864	6,479	3,867
1959	7,812	4,339	4,489	2,806
1960	6,439	3,627	6,362	3,877
1961	6,243	3,540	4,473	2,830
1962	4,386	2,546	8,946	5,500
1963	6,249	3,444	9,099	5,449

TABLE F-2

Average Capital Gains: Small Manufacturing Sample, 1940–63; Extreme Stockholdings Deleted
(amounts in dollars)

Year	Top Executive		Top Five Executives	
	Before Taxes	After Taxes	Before Taxes	After Taxes
1940	−15,728	−13,369	−7,425	−6,311
1941	−178,489	−151,716	−43,991	−37,392
1942	68,288	58,045	20,460	17,391
1943	158,353	134,600	38,952	33,109
1944	139,015	118,163	40,519	34,441
1945	133,124	113,155	42,720	36,312
1946	−95,192	−80,913	−28,718	−24,410
1947	−130,174	−110,648	−25,946	−22,054
1948	−53,031	−45,076	−15,352	−13,049
1949	9,840	8,364	3,148	2,676
1950	34,132	29,012	9,535	8,105
1951	−1,766	−1,501	1,688	1,435
1952	22,142	18,821	5,333	4,533
1953	−21,466	−18,246	−5,461	−4,642
1954	58,569	49,784	20,158	17,134
1955	14,128	12,009	8,794	7,475
1956	60,859	51,730	22,867	19,437
1957	−76,841	−65,315	−23,287	−19,794
1958	175,744	149,382	51,360	43,656
1959	24,258	20,619	14,079	11,967
1960	−17,413	−14,801	896	762
1961	69,365	58,960	38,468	32,698
1962	−15,299	−13,004	−20,085	−17,072
1963	46,574	39,588	47,886	40,703

TABLE F-3

Average Absolute Capital Gains: Small Manufacturing Sample,
1940–63; Extreme Stockholdings Deleted
(amounts in dollars)

	Top Executive		Top Five Executives	
Year	Before Taxes	After Taxes	Before Taxes	After Taxes
1940	88,345	75,093	22,576	19,190
1941	192,128	163,309	47,444	40,327
1942	71,978	61,181	22,176	18,850
1943	158,353	134,600	38,952	33,109
1944	139,152	118,279	40,602	34,512
1945	133,124	113,155	42,720	36,312
1946	103,925	88,336	32,580	27,693
1947	144,087	122,474	31,841	27,065
1948	54,593	46,404	16,516	14,039
1949	27,199	23,119	8,645	7,348
1950	41,739	35,478	11,851	10,073
1951	15,034	12,779	7,969	6,774
1952	23,689	20,136	6,811	5,789
1953	22,689	19,286	7,481	6,359
1954	58,569	49,784	20,158	17,134
1955	47,095	40,031	18,286	15,543
1956	72,494	61,620	27,532	23,402
1957	80,342	68,291	24,220	20,587
1958	175,744	149,382	51,360	43,656
1959	44,274	37,633	19,231	16,346
1960	25,154	21,381	27,800	23,630
1961	74,265	63,125	41,882	35,600
1962	25,141	21,370	43,832	37,257
1963	49,066	41,706	54,599	46,409

TABLE F-4

Average Total After-Tax Compensation: Small Manufacturing
Sample, 1940–63; Extreme Values Deleted
(amounts in dollars)

Year	Top Executive	Top Five Executives
1940	33,290	23,299
1941	33,201	21,855
1942	28,037	19,835
1943	24,536	17,433
1944	25,588	17,749
1945	25,746	19,163
1946	30,877	22,092
1947	33,287	25,449
1948	41,788	30,714
1949	49,589	32,245
1950	46,927	32,279
1951	44,195	32,674
1952	44,472	32,370
1953	49,784	37,149
1954	54,173	36,981
1955	58,788	39,665
1956	76,064	44,667
1957	60,117	41,428
1958	60,153	41,494
1959	66,889	47,220
1960	70,165	51,251
1961	62,936	48,394
1962	77,486	53,166
1963	61,120	45,804

BIBLIOGRAPHY

A. Books

Baker, John C., *Executive Salaries and Bonus Plans.* New York: McGraw-Hill, 1938.

Baumol, William J., *Business Behavior, Value, and Growth,* rev. ed. New York: Macmillan, 1967.

Berle, Adolf A., and Means, Gardiner C., *The Modern Corporation and Private Property.* New York: Macmillan, 1934.

Burgess, Leonard R., *Top Executive Pay Package.* New York: Free Press, 1963.

Galbraith, John K., *The New Industrial State.* Boston: Houghton-Mifflin, 1967.

Gordon, Myron J., *The Investment, Financing, and Valuation of the Corporation.* Homewood, Ill.: Irwin, 1962.

Gordon, Robert A., *Business Leadership in the Large Corporation.* Berkeley: University of California Press, 1961.

Hall, Challis A., *Effects of Taxation on Executive Compensation and Retirement Plans.* Cambridge, Mass.: Riverside Press, 1951.

Lewellen, Wilbur G., *Executive Compensation in Large Industrial Corporations.* New York: National Bureau of Economic Research, 1968.

Lutz, Friedrich, and Lutz, Vera, *The Theory of Investment of the Firm.* Princeton: Princeton University Press, 1951.

Marris, Robin, *The Economic Theory of Managerial Capitalism.* New York: Free Press, 1964.

Patton, Arch., *Men, Money, and Motivation.* New York: McGraw-Hill, 1961.

Roberts, David R., *Executive Compensation.* New York: Free Press, 1959.

Washington, George T., and Rothschild, V. Henry, *Corporate Executives' Compensation.* New York: Ronald Press, 1942 (title changed to *Compensating the Corporate Executive* for 2nd and 3rd eds., 1951 and 1962).

Williamson, Oliver E., *The Economics of Discretionary Behavior.* Englewood Cliffs, N.J.: Prentice-Hall, 1964.

B. Publications of the Government

U.S. Bureau of the Census, *Statistical Abstract of the United States: 1965*. Washington, D.C.: U.S. Government Printing Office, 1965.

U.S. Department of Commerce, *Survey of Current Business*. Washington, D.C.: U.S. Government Printing Office, August 1949, January 1950, July 1950, July 1951, July 1952, December 1956, May 1965.

U.S. Department of Labor, Bureau of Labor Statistics, *Employment and Earnings Statistics for the United States: 1909–1964* (Bulletin No. 1312-2). Washington, D.C.: U.S. Government Printing Office, 1964.

U.S. Joint Economic Committee, *The Federal Tax System: Facts and Problems*. Washington, D.C.: U.S. Government Printing Office, 1964.

U.S. Securities and Exchange Commission, *Official Summary of Security Transactions and Holdings*, Vols. 5–30. Washington, D.C.: U.S. Government Printing Office, 1939–1964.

U.S. Treasury Department, Internal Revenue Service, *Statistics of Income: Individual Tax Returns*. Washington, D.C.: U.S. Government Printing Office, 1944, 1947, 1950, 1953, 1956, 1959.

C. Periodicals

Baumol, William J., "On the Theory of Oligopoly," *Economica*, Vol. XXV, No. 99 (August 1958), pp. 187–198.

———, "On the Theory of Expansion of the Firm," *American Economic Review*, Vol. LII, No. 5 (December 1962), pp. 1078–1087.

Commerce Clearing House, *Standard Federal Tax Reporter*, New York, 1960–1965.

Durand, David, "Costs of Debt and Equity Funds for Business: Trends and Problems of Measurement," *Conference on Research in Business Finance*. New York: National Bureau of Economic Research, 1952, pp. 215–247.

Edwards, Charles E., and Hilton, James G., "A Note on the High-Low Price Average as an Estimator of Annual Average Stock Prices," *Journal of Finance*, Vol. XXI, No. 1 (March 1966), pp. 112–115.

Fortune, "The Fortune Directory," Vol. 70, No. 1 (July 1964), pp. 179–198.

———, "The Fortune Directory: Part II," Vol. 70, No. 2 (August 1964), pp. 151–162.

Gordon, Robert A., "Ownership and Compensation as Incentives to Corporate Executives," *Quarterly Journal of Economics,* Vol. LIV, No. 2 (May 1940), pp. 455–473.

Holland, Daniel M., and Lewellen, Wilbur G., "Probing the Record of Stock Options," *Harvard Business Review,* Vol. 40, No. 2 (March–April 1962), pp. 132–150.

Larner, Robert J., "Ownership and Control in the 200 Largest Non-financial Corporations, 1929 and 1963," *American Economic Review,* Vol. LVI, No. 4 (September 1966), pp. 777–787.

Lewellen, Wilbur G., "Executives Lose Out, Even With Options," *Harvard Business Review,* Vol. 46, No. 1 (January–February 1968), pp. 127–142.

———, "Management and Ownership in the Large Firm," *Journal of Finance,* Vol. XXIV, No. 2 (May 1969), pp. 299–322.

———, and Huntsman, Blaine, "Managerial Pay and Corporate Performance," *American Economic Review,* Vol. LX, No. 4 (September 1970).

Lintner, John, "Optimal Dividends and Corporate Growth Under Uncertainty," *Quarterly Journal of Economics,* Vol. LXXVIII, No. 1 (February 1964), pp. 49–95.

———, "The Valuation of Risk Assets and the Selection of Risky Investments in Stock Portfolios and Capital Budgets," *Review of Economics and Statistics,* Vol. LVII, No. 1 (February 1965), pp. 13–37.

McGuire, Joseph W., Chiu, John S., and Elbing, Alvar O., "Executive Incomes, Sales, and Profits," *American Economic Review,* Vol. LII, No. 4 (September 1962), pp. 753–761.

Mason, Edward J., "The Apologetics of Managerialism," *Journal of Business,* Vol. XXXI, No. 1 (January 1958), pp. 1–11.

Modigliani, Franco, and Miller, Merton H., "The Cost of Capital, Corporation Finance, and the Theory of Investment," *American Economic Review,* Vol. XLVIII, No. 3 (June 1958), pp. 261–297.

Monsen, R. Joseph, Chiu, John S., and Cooley, David E., "The Effect of Separation of Ownership and Control on the Performance of the Large Firm," *Quarterly Journal of Economics,* Vol. LXXXII, No. 3 (August 1968), pp. 435–451.

Moody's Industrial Manual, 1940–1964. New York: Moody's Investor's Service.

Poor's Register of Corporations, Directors, and Executives, 1952–1964. New York: Standard and Poor's Corporation.

Who's Who in America, Vols. 21–33. Chicago: Marquis–Who's Who, 1940–1964.

Williamson, J., "Growth, Sales, and Profit Maximization," *Economica,* Vol. XXXIII, No. 129 (February 1966), pp. 1–16.

Williamson, Oliver E., "Managerial Discretion and Business Behavior," *American Economic Review,* Vol. LIII, No. 5 (December 1963), pp. 1032–1057.

World Who's Who in Commerce and Industry, Vols. 3–13. Chicago: Marquis–Who's Who, 1940–1965.

INDEX

INDEX